The Personal Correspondence

of Hildegard of Bingen

The Personal Correspondence of
Hildegard of Bingen

SELECTED LETTERS WITH AN INTRODUCTION
AND COMMENTARY BY *Joseph L. Baird*

The letters in this volume are selected from
The Letters of Hildegard of Bingen *(3 vols.),*
translated by Joseph L. Baird and Radd K. Ehrman

UNIVERSITY PRESS

2006

OXFORD
UNIVERSITY PRESS

Oxford University Press, Inc., publishes works that further
Oxford University's objective of excellence
in research, scholarship, and education.

Oxford   New York
Auckland   Cape Town   Dar es Salaam   Hong Kong   Karachi
Kuala Lumpur   Madrid   Melbourne   Mexico City   Nairobi
New Delhi   Shanghai   Taipei   Toronto

With offices in
Argentina   Austria   Brazil   Chile   Czech Republic   France   Greece
Guatemala   Hungary   Italy   Japan   Poland   Portugal   Singapore
South Korea   Switzerland   Thailand   Turkey   Ukraine   Vietnam

Copyright © 2006 by Oxford University Press, Inc.

The letters in this volume are reprinted from *The Letters of Hildegard of Bingen* (3 vols.)
translated by Joseph L. Baird and Radd K. Ehrman.
Volume I: Copyright © 1994 by Oxford University Press, Inc.
Volume II: Copyright © 1998 by Oxford University Press, Inc.
Volume III: Copyright © 2004 by Oxford University Press, Inc.

Published by Oxford University Press, Inc.
198 Madison Avenue, New York, New York 10016

www.oup.com

Oxford is a registered trademark of Oxford University Press

All rights reserved. No part of this publication may be reproduced,
stored in a retrieval system, or transmitted, in any form or by any means,
electronic, mechanical, photocopying, recording, or otherwise,
without the prior permission of Oxford University Press.

Library of Congress Cataloging-in-Publication Data
Hildegard, Saint, 1098–1179.
  [Correspondence. English. Selections]
  The personal correspondence of Hildegard of Bingen / Selected Letters with an
Introduction and Commentary by Joseph L. Baird.
     p. cm.
  "The letters in this volume are selected from The Letters of Hildegard of Bingen
(3 vols.) translated by Joseph L. Baird and Radd K. Ehrman."
  Includes bibliographical references and indexes.
  ISBN-13 978-0-19-530822-8; 978-0-19-530823-5 (pbk.)
  ISBN 0-19-530822-0; 0-19-530823-9 (pbk.)
  1. Hildegard, Saint, 1098–1179—Correspondence.   2. Christian saints—
Germany—Correspondence.   I. Baird, Joseph L.   II. Title.
  BX4700.H5A4 2006
  282.092—dc22   2006005026

9 8 7 6 5 4 3 2 1

Printed in the United States of America
on acid-free paper

*To my daughter Eve,
that other tough, spiritual lady*

Acknowledgments

I would like to express my appreciation to the following people: First and foremost to my daughter Eve, who listened, early on, to my prose in progress, and, later on, read every word of the manuscript; to Rob James, for his interest and encouragement; to Herb Story, for his assistance in last-minute checking; to Jan Bennett, Steve Staub, and Sherril Gerard, for their responsive listening to my reading of the introduction, followed by animated discussion; and, finally, to Jim Jagers, who also listened patiently, exclaiming from time to time, incredulously, "Did *you* write that?" Appreciation is, of course, also due to Professor Radd Ehrman, longtime colleague (collaborator, friend), with whom I worked closely for nigh onto two decades to produce the translation of the complete body of Hildegard's correspondence.

Contents

Table of Letters   xiii

Introduction   3

Chapter 1: Reaching Out   15

    Letter 1   to Bernard of Clairvaux   17
    Letter 2   from Bernard of Clairvaux   20
    Letter 3   to Pope Eugenius III   21

Chapter 2: Criticism and Response   23

    Letter 4   from Mistress Tengswich   24
    Letter 5   to Mistress Tengswich   26
    Letter 6   to the Abbot of Mount St. Disibod   30
    Letter 7   from Adelbert, Prior at Mount St. Disibod   30
    Letter 8   to Helengerus, Abbot of Mount St. Disibod   32
    Letter 9   from Helengerus, Abbot of Mount St. Disibod   33
    Letter 10   to Her Own Community   35

Chapter 3: Richardis von Stade   39

    Letter 11   to the Margravine Richardis von Stade   41
    Letter 12   from Heinrich, Archbishop of Mainz   41
    Letter 13   to Heinrich, Archbishop of Mainz   42
    Letter 14   to Hartwig, Archbishop of Bremen   43
    Letter 15   from Pope Eugenius III   45
    Letter 16   to Richardis   47
    Letter 17   from Hartwig, Archbishop of Bremen   48
    Letter 18   to Hartwig, Archbishop of Bremen   49
    Letter 19   from the Abbess Adelheid   51

CONTENTS

Chapter 4: Hildegard's Spreading Reputation   53

    Letter 20   from Odo of Soissons   54
    Letter 21   to Odo of Soissons   55
    Letter 22   from a Provost   56
    Letter 23   from Godfrey the Monk   57
    Letter 24   to the Monk Godfrey   59
    Letter 25   to Gero, Bishop of Halberstadt   59
    Letter 26   to a Widow   60
    Letter 27   to Luthgard of Karlsburg   61
    Letter 28   to Sibyl, a Married Woman of Lausanne   61
    Letter 29   to a Cleric   62
    Letter 30   to a Priest   62
    Letter 31   from a Provisor   63
    Letter 32   to Rudeger, a Monk   64
    Letter 33   to Manegold, Abbot of Hirsau   66
    Letter 34   to a Person Seeking Treasure   67
    Letter 35   to a Certain Person   67
    Letter 36   to a Former Nun   68
    Letter 37   to the Nun Luitburga   70
    Letter 38   to a Community of Monks   70
    Letter 39   to a Prelate   71
    Letter 40   to an Abbess   72
    Letter 41   from the Priest Baldemar   74
    Letter 42   from a Priest   76
    Letter 43   from Frederick Barbarossa   77
    Letter 44   to Frederick Barbarossa   78
    Letter 45   to Frederick Barbarossa   78
    Letter 46   to Eleanor of Aquitaine   78
    Letter 47   from a Provost   79

Chapter 5: Exorcism 80

    Letter 48   to the Abbot, Gedolphus   80
    Letter 49   from Gedolphus   84
    Letter 50   to a Dean   85
    Appendix to Letter 50   86

Chapter 6: Family 92

    Letter 51   from Arnold, Archbishop of Trier   92
    Letter 52   to Arnold, Archbishop of Trier   94
    Letter 53   to Her Brother Hugo   96

Chapter 7: A Fellow Visionary 97

    Letter 54   from Elisabeth of Schönau   98
    Letter 55   to Elisabeth of Schönau   103

Chapter 8: A Sermon 106

    Letter 56   from the Clerics of Cologne   106
    Letter 57   to the Clerics of Cologne   107

Chapter 9: The Provost Volmar 117

    Letter 58   from the Provost Volmar   117
    Letter 59   to Pope Alexander III   120
    Letter 60   from Pope Alexander III   122

Chapter 10: Miscellaneous Letters and Visions 123

    Letter 61   to an Abbot   123
    Letter 62   to a Teacher   124
    Letter 63   Vision of a Soul in Purgatory   126
    Letter 64   Vision of the Soul of a Certain Sinner   127
    Letter 65   Satan's Rape of the First Woman   128

CONTENTS

    Letter 66   from Ludwig, Abbot of St. Eucharius   130
    Letter 67   to Ludwig, Abbot of St. Eucharius   131
    Letter 68   to Ludwig, Abbot of St. Eucharius   132
    Letter 69   a Message   133

Chapter 11: Guibert of Gembloux   135

    Letter 70   to Guibert of Gembloux   136
    Letter 71   from Guibert of Gembloux   142

Chapter 12: The Last, Bitter Controversy   155

    Letter 72   to the Prelates at Mainz   156
    Letter 73   to Christian, Archbishop of Mainz   162
    Letter 74   from Christian, Archbishop of Mainz   164

Chapter 13: Songs and Hymns   167

    Letter 75   A Meditation   167

Select Bibliography   187

Index   189

Table of Letters

In the following list, the numbers in bold are the letter numbers in this volume. Those to the right of these are the corresponding letters in the standard edition/translation.

1	1	**20**	39	**39**	264	**58**	195
2	1r	**21**	39r	**40**	268	**59**	10
3	2	**22**	165	**41**	295	**60**	10r
4	52	**23**	48	**42**	297	**61**	258
5	52r	**24**	48r	**43**	314	**62**	280
6	75	**25**	33	**44**	315	**63**	376
7	78	**26**	356	**45**	313	**64**	369
8	76r	**27**	336	**46**	318	**65**	375
9	77	**28**	338	**47**	154	**66**	215
10	195r	**29**	309	**48**	68r	**67**	215r
11	323	**30**	293	**49**	69	**68**	217
12	18	**31**	114	**50**	158r	**69**	382
13	18r	**32**	89	**51**	27	**70**	103r
14	12	**33**	131	**52**	27r	**71**	104
15	4	**34**	358	**53**	208	**72**	23
16	64	**35**	364	**54**	201	**73**	24
17	13	**36**	354	**55**	201r	**74**	24r
18	13r	**37**	222	**56**	15	**75**	390
19	100	**38**	219	**57**	15r		

xiii

*The Personal Correspondence
of Hildegard of Bingen*

Introduction

In 1106, when she was eight years old, Hildegard was enclosed—for life—in a small cell on the grounds of a monastery of Benedictine monks at Mount St. Disibod, a short distance from her birthplace and the home of her parents. She was placed in the care, and under the tutelage, of an older, yet still relatively young, recluse, one Jutta of Sponheim, who as a young woman had insisted on the life of an anchorite. Evidence for the little hermitage at St. Disibod is quite meager, but other sources from the Middle Ages give us what is likely a reasonably accurate picture of the situation there. The structure in which the two were to live out their lives would have had one door, locked from the outside, and one window, through which they received their food and passed out their refuse. At the entry into such a life, a solemn liturgical ceremony was performed, with the rites of the dead being read over the entrants. For they were, henceforth, considered as dead to this world, destined to live out the brief moment of this life in paradisal seclusion from the evils of the outside world to insure their eternal life in the world beyond.

And that was that!

With Hildegard entombed for life at the age of eight.

Whose "brief moment" lived in seclusion would have been seventy-three years, since she lived to be eighty-one.

Whose days from that point forward were to be spent on attending her psalter and concentrating on her interior religious life.

That was the way it was supposed to be. That was the way it started out.

Yet this is the woman whom we later see traveling throughout Germany, making four long and arduous journeys to preach to the people, a woman preaching to, of all things, exclusively male audiences, as well as to the general populace.

This is the woman who was invited to the palace of the great Emperor, Frederick I, Barbarossa, where she made certain prophecies to her imperial host.

This is the woman who as head of her own monastery, surrounded by her chorus of nuns, dressed those lovely young ladies in the finery of paradise, with flowing tresses and flowing white garments that reached to their feet, and with golden crowns on their heads—to the dismay of some religious conservatives of the time.

This is the woman who produced and staged an elaborate morality play, for which she wrote both words and music—the first of its kind, inventing the form.

This is the woman who founded two separate monasteries in her own right, with herself as head.

This is the woman whom priests consulted about peculiarly male prerogatives and fields of inquiry, how to conduct Mass properly and how to resolve certain esoteric religious mysteries.

This is the woman who wrote three major books of striking originality of thought and image.

This is the woman who knew and corresponded with many of the most important people of her time: with Eleanor of Aquitaine,

INTRODUCTION

that other high-spirited woman of the Middle Ages, with Henry II of England, with Frederick Barbarossa, with four different popes, with the Empress Irene of Greece, with archbishops and dukes and monks and, in some ways most significant of all, with people of no particular importance whatsoever—which is what this book is about.

Quite a set of accomplishments for a "dead" woman!

How could this have happened? Just what caused this "resurrection" of Hildegard from the dead? As with so many events so far removed in time, the evidence is very scanty. What we do know is this: the fame of the sanctity of those two recluses (presumably Jutta, rather than Hildegard, at this early stage) spread abroad very quickly, and other noble young ladies began suing for entry into their community. Certain logical conclusions follow from this fact: as the number of those seeking admission increased, the monks would have had to enlarge the quarters in which they were to be housed, and, let us be clear, the monks had solid financial, as well as holy, incentives to make such accommodations. These young ladies came with dowries, a sordid matter Hildegard would have to deal with once she established her own independent community, as can be followed in the correspondence. In any case, the growth in numbers would have totally subverted the original plan, with the former straitened cell being transformed into a full-fledged convent of Benedictine nuns, and with such a change, as the end result forces us to conclude, came the gradual relaxation of the earlier restrictions.

But let us return for a moment to that small cell where the two are enclosed. On thinking of the situation there, certain questions nag at the back of the mind of any but the most dry-as-dust, disengaged scholar. What was it like for a little girl to be incarcerated in such a fashion? There is, of course, no real way to answer that question, not even if we had a confirming document from the Middle Ages, for all such medieval prequels to a saint's life present their subjects as insufferable little prigs who always dutifully attend to their prayers and pious obligations. Still, it is sometimes worthwhile to ask the unanswerable questions, if only to refocus the mind and give flesh and life to these otherwise bloodless creatures. Did high animal spirits sometimes course through the veins of the little girl and cause her to dance delightedly about in the narrow confines of that little domicile? Did Jutta sometimes have to smack her and grumble, "Attend to your psalter, girl"? Did the young Hildegard sometimes gaze longingly out that single window and wish to run out in the meadows and chase a butterfly she saw at a distance? Did, at some time, the stark realization of what "for life" meant come fleetingly into her consciousness? On this last point we may have a pertinent letter (#36) if we read carefully between the lines. Many years later, Hildegard learned of a nun who had broken all her vows and returned to a secular life, giving as an excuse that she had been forced to take the veil against her will. Hildegard sits down immediately and writes a fiery letter to the lapsed nun threatening her with all the pangs of hell if she does not return to her former blessed state, and this despite the fact (for she refers to it in her letter) that the person was brought into the state (in childhood perhaps, like Hildegard?) without her consent. Of course, as a nun herself, and in charge of nuns, Hildegard may have felt compelled to write such a letter in any case, but what is shocking is the fierceness of the threatened punishment, without any alleviation, from a woman who is usually merciful to even the most flagrant sinner. Does this letter, then, reflect somehow on her own childhood experience?

We do, I think, have at least one small bit of information about the mutual relationships between the two in their cloistered setting. In the beginning, the young Hildegard would have been shy and restrained in her relationship with Jutta, keeping her own little secret to herself, for she had learned to be guarded in her contact with other people. Hildegard herself tells us that she began

INTRODUCTION

receiving visions as early as the age of three, and that she saw "things" in her spirit, while at the same time she saw with her physical eyes. Not knowing at the time that other people had no such vision, she spoke openly of such matters—until she was taken aback by their response. Then in order to confirm her growing suspicion that she was somehow different, she says, "I asked a nurse of mine if she saw things other than with her physical eyes, and she gave me no answer since she saw nothing of them." After this, she informs us, she became very wary and attempted to conceal such things from other people. This must have been the way it was at first in her relationship with Jutta, until she gained confidence and began to put her trust in her tutor and companion. This is a reasonable assessment, surely, of the young Hildegard's reluctance to share her gift with anyone, for that reluctance is still there some forty years later.

In 1146 or 1147, Hildegard made her first attempt to gain ecclesiastical approval of her visionary experience. She wrote the then famous and influential Bernard of Clairvaux—later to become St. Bernard—and in the course of the letter she indicates that only "a certain monk" was privy to the secret of her visions. By this time Jutta had been dead for some ten years, with Hildegard now serving as abbess of the community. That "certain monk" was Volmar of St. Disibod, Hildegard's spiritual adviser, confidant, secretary, and friend—who was to remain so for over thirty years. Save for the letter to Bernard, the chronological sequence of Hildegard's "coming out" as a visionary is quite murky, but the basic facts are unquestioned. At some point Hildegard took Jutta into her confidence, and Jutta shared those revelations with Volmar. Eventually, the pope gets the word, and, from there, the world. No need for further explanation here. The participants in the events speak for themselves in the following correspondence, with accompanying headnotes to place the letters in context. As can be seen from the date above, long years have passed since the little eight-year-old

7

was enclosed for life. It is startling to realize, especially considering the volume and variety of work she produced, that Hildegard was forty-eight or forty-nine before she reached out to the larger world, and, as an interesting aside, she did not become Hildegard *of Bingen* until she was fifty-two, for that was when she left her home monastery to establish her own community on a hill overlooking the juncture of the Nahe and Rhine Rivers at a place called Bingen.

But what was the nature of Hildegard's visionary experience? Perhaps it is best to let her speak for herself. In the *Scivias*, she gives the following account:

> And again I heard a voice from heaven saying to me:
> "Speak of these wonders, therefore, and write and say them in the way you were taught."
>
> It came to pass in the eleven hundred and forty-first year of the incarnation of the Son of God, Jesus Christ, when I was forty-two years and seven months old, heaven opened up, and a fiery light, piercingly bright, penetrated my entire brain, and like a warming flame that does not burn, that light inflamed all my heart and breast, just as the sun's rays warm anything they touch. And immediately I knew the meaning of the exposition of the Scriptures, that is to say, of the psalter, the gospel, and other Catholic volumes of both the Old and the New Testaments—but not the interpretation of the words of their texts, neither the division into syllables nor the recognition of cases and tenses. Yet as at that time of my illumination, I have sensed in myself the power and mystery of secret and wonderful visions from my earliest childhood, as early as five years old,[1] and I still do. Still, I did

---

1. Well, sometimes Hildegard gets confused (so nice to see in a saint!) about her early childhood. Sometimes she says it was at the age of three.

INTRODUCTION

not tell anyone about these marvelous things, except to certain ones who lived in the same religious state as I did. But I kept all of this quiet within myself, in the meantime, until the time when God in His grace wished it to be revealed. And these visions that I saw? I did not see them in dreams while sleeping or in a delirious state, nor did I see them with the bodily eyes or hear them with the exterior ears, nor did I perceive them in hidden places. I saw them only when wide awake in complete command of my senses, with the eyes and ears of the interior being, in open places, according to the will of God. How this could possibly be is difficult for carnal man to understand.[2]

It would be superfluous in a work of this kind to give an accounting of all of Hildegard's various books, but a brief remark and quotation from the *Scivias* will focus more sharply on what Hildegard means by her celestial visions. The title *Scivias* itself is apparently a Latin portmanteau word that stands for *Scito vias [Dei]*, "Know the Ways [of God]," an apt title for a work that is concerned with an explanation of those ways of God throughout all of salvation history. Hildegard's method is, first of all, to meticulously describe a vision she has received from her celestial source, and, then, to explicate that vision down to the minutest detail. There are twenty-six such visions in the entire book,[3] and here is the first vision of Book Two:

> Behold, I—a female person not vibrant with the strength
> of strong lions and not taught by their inspiration, but

---

2. Save for the letters, all translations from the Latin are my own. Translations of the letters are the fully collaborative effort of Radd Ehrman and myself, published earlier in three volumes by Oxford University Press.

3. A manuscript of the *Scivias* prepared in Hildegard's own scriptorium, presumably under her supervision, contained invaluable illuminations, but during World War II it was sent up to Dresden (for safekeeping!), and has been missing since 1945. Fortunately, some twenty years before, the nuns had made a handwritten and hand-painted copy.

9

only a tender and fragile rib infused by a mystical breath—I saw a blazing fire, incomprehensible, inextinguishable, totally living and totally Life, and this fire contained within itself another flame of the color of the ethereal air, which burned avidly with a light wind, and it was as inseparable from that first blazing fire as the viscera are in a human being. And I saw that that flame flashed like lightning and blazed up. And, behold, suddenly a dark spheroid of ambient air of great magnitude came forth from nothing. And that flame hovered over it and struck it repeatedly, striking sparks from it, until that rounded air was brought through to full perfection so that heaven and earth were fully formed and resplendent. Then that flame within the blazing fire, and in the burning of it, extended itself out to a little clod of mud lying in the deep, and warmed it so that it became flesh and blood, and breathed on it so that it rose up a living being. After this was done, through the flame which burned avidly with a light wind, that bright fire presented to the man a perfectly white flower, which hung in that flame just as dew hangs on the grass. The sweet odor of this flower reached the man's nostrils, but he did not taste it with his mouth or touch it with his hands, and so turned himself away and fell into the deepest darkness, and could not pull himself up. And that darkness grew more and more intense, spreading itself out in that air. Then three large stars, their brilliant light mingling together, appeared in that darkness, and, afterward, many others, both large and small, shining with great splendor. Then, at last, there appeared an enormous star, radiating with wondrous brightness and sending its rays to that flame. And also on the earth there appeared a radiance like the dawn, into which that flame was miraculously absorbed, while still

INTRODUCTION

not being separated from that blazing fire. And so in the radiance of that dawn, the Supreme Will was enkindled.

In her letter to Guibert of Gembloux (number 69), Hildegard describes her means of "seeing" at great length.

Two minor works of Hildegard's deserve notice here, merely because they are so mysterious—and fascinating. She refers to the divine inspiration for the two in a letter to Pope Anastasius III, written in 1153 or 1154. She writes: "But He Who is great and without flaw has now touched a humble dwelling, so that it might see a miracle and form unknown letters and utter an unknown tongue. And this was said to that little habitation: 'You have written these things in a language given to you from above, rather than in ordinary human speech, since it was not revealed to you in that form, but let him who has the pumice stone not fail to polish it and make it intelligible to mankind.'" The reference is to the two modest works, essentially mere lists, which go under the titles of *Lingua ignota*, "Unknown Language," and *Litterae ignotae*, "Unknown Letters." The latter is a fabricated, new alphabet. More intriguing is the *Lingua ignota*, which is composed of a list of slightly over a thousand invented words; it is like a golden vocabulary chain extending from the heights of heaven to the lowest reaches of earth, stretching from the godhead to the mundane world of the lowly grasshopper. Some of the fabricated terms seem to have an underlying allegorical meaning, as in the word for God, *aigonz*, which moves solemnly from the "alpha" to the "omega," or, rather, in the Roman alphabet, to "zed" ("I am the beginning and the end"), and the word for Christ, *liuionz*, extending from "ell," that is, the middle of the alphabet, to "zed" once again. But it is unclear to what purpose this invented language was dedicated, and there is only one known instance of Hildegard's employment of it. In a song Hildegard composed to celebrate the divine institution of the Church, she blithely uses five of the words, without comment or gloss, a verse that can be seen in the last document of this volume.

Hildegard was absolutely assured of her place, her prophetic role, in Christian history. In an autobiographical section of the *Vita*, she writes that "in the eleven hundredth year after the Incarnation of Christ, the teaching and fiery justice of the Apostles, which Christ had established among the Christians and spiritual people, began to slow down and to turn into hesitation." Then, without the slightest hesitation on her own part, she adds immediately, "I was born in those times." That time period, as she is to say again and again in the correspondence and in her larger works, was a weak, effeminate time. The virile part of the Church had grown effete and womanish, and, paradoxically, God had called the weak to confound the strong. Hildegard always keeps the stress on herself as a "poor little form of a woman," a phrase she repeats over and over again. But she relies on the paradox. Unlike in the visionary works where it was to be expected, one is sometimes startled to see in the correspondence the personal "me" transformed into the transcendent "Me," the voice of the Living Light speaking through the poor effeminate form.

Material about the life of Hildegard is more generous than for most figures from the Middle Ages. She herself wrote rather extensively about her own life in letters and in prefaces to her various books. Moreover, there were three different writers who, in the second half of the twelfth century, set out to record the events of her life, one during her own lifetime, and the others shortly thereafter. After the death of Volmar in 1173, Gottfried of St. Disibod became provost of Mount St. Rupert and secretary to Hildegard, and he took advantage of his position to write a biography. Unfortunately, that gratifying effort was left incomplete by Gottfried's early death. A short time after Hildegard's own death in 1179, Theodoric of Echternach took up and completed Gottfried's work. Theodoric's part of the biography is especially noteworthy, for he quotes extensively from some otherwise unknown autobiographical material by Hildegard. This work—that is, Gottfried's as completed by Theodoric—is generally, as in this volume, known as the *Vita*. Also,

INTRODUCTION

Guibert of Gembloux, Hildegard's last secretary, wrote a somewhat truncated biography, for reasons unknown taking the story of her life only up to the move from Mount St. Disibod in 1150, and, therefore, annoyingly, repeating information already known, although he was with her up through her death and could have been very informative about her later years. The so-called *Acta*, containing the material gathered in support of her canonization, also survives, but it is filled with legendary tales about miracles and healings and has little worth as biographical information. Further evidence survives in the form of chronicles and official documents, such as those dealing with the two monasteries that Hildegard founded.

Despite these indications of her reputation and fame in her own age, Hildegard of Bingen was almost lost to history. For century after century, those who even recognized her name would have been very scarce indeed. It was left to the twentieth century to rediscover this extraordinary woman, particularly with the work of Peter Dronke, which came as late as the 1980s. Nowadays, especially in the field of music, her work is widely acclaimed. Her music, which was inventive and out of the mainstream of her own time, has been revived and played to appreciative audiences worldwide. And recorded on compact disc, doubtless to the amusement of Hildegard's spirit. Curiously, in the 1980s and 1990s she was picked up by the New Age people and became a kind of cult figure among those groups. Hildegard's longer works, such as the *Scivias*, are scarcely read, of course, outside of scholarly circles, but they—particularly the *Scivias*—would be a rewarding experience for anyone of a religious or mystical temperament. But perhaps Barbara Newman, one of the most notable Hildegard scholars, has best summed up Hildegard's present-day reputation. In the introduction to Hart and Bishop's translation of the *Scivias*, she writes:

> In our own day the voice that Hildegard had called "a small sound of the trumpet from the living Light" is resounding

once more. In Germany she still enjoys a wide popular cult, and the abbey at Eibingen[4] has become a center of scholarship and pilgrimage. Herbalists have rediscovered some of her prescriptions and begun to experiment with their use in modern homeopathic practice. Musicians have performed her liturgical songs and her drama, the *Ordo virtutum*, to great acclaim. To students of spirituality Hildegard remains of compelling interest, not only as a rare feminine voice soaring above the patriarchal choirs, but also as a perfect embodiment of the integrated, holistic approach to God and humanity for which our fragmented era longs. While the movement for creation-centered spirituality has exaggerated certain elements of her teaching and denied its more ascetic and dualist aspects, it remains true that Hildegard unites vision with doctrine, religion with science, charismatic jubilation with prophetic indignation, and the longing for social order with the quest for social justice in ways that continue to challenge and inspire.

My own scholarly work with Hildegard began nearly three decades ago, and in touching those documents, I soon found that I was touching a living human being. And that is what the reader will find here in her personal correspondence, a saint, to be sure, but a saint with all her personal foibles and idiosyncrasies, a woman who sorrows and hurts; who is compassionate and tender, yet unshakable on principle; who is vulnerable as a poor little form of a woman and absolutely unyielding as the voice of the Living Light. Hildegard was, clearly, the most remarkable woman—one is tempted to say *person*—of the Middle Ages, and, in a large sense, she too was not for an age but for all time.

---

4. Now the Abbey of St. Hildegard, this is the second monastery that Hildegard founded; the first, St. Rupert, was destroyed during the Thirty Years' War.

Reaching Out

At some point in the year 1146 or 1147, a quiet little scene was taking place in the cloister at Mount St. Disibod. The woman to be known to history as Hildegard of Bingen sat in her small scriptorium composing a letter. And since this was a letter of the greatest import, one on which she must have felt her whole future depended, she was probably accompanied by the devoted monk Volmar, her faithful secretary, whose duty it was to see to the proper cases and numbers of that difficult Latin language that Hildegard never quite mastered. Likely present also would have been the young nun, Richardis von Stade, Hildegard's beloved assistant and companion.[1] The moment was quiet at this time, the voice subdued, but this little scene presaged the celestial thunder that soon was to echo forth from Hildegard's place of residence.

This letter, a plea for the recognition of her divine gift, was addressed to the saintly and politically powerful Bernard of Clairvaux.

---

1. An illumination in a thirteenth-century manuscript depicts Hildegard with wax tablet in hand. On the other side sits Volmar copying the corrected text, while a nun stands nearby ready to offer assistance.

It is the very first letter of Hildegard's voluminous correspondence that has come down to us, and, as the letter itself suggests, this appears to be the first time that Hildegard has cast her voice abroad, beyond the bounds of her cloistered setting. Hesitant and faltering in tone, the letter, with its stress on feminine humility and its open admiration for the correspondent, is nicely calculated to gain the aid of this influential prelate, who, Hildegard must have known, had the ear of the pope. The diffident, self-effacing manner here contrasts sharply with the forceful tones of the voice of the Living Light that Hildegard adopts only a short time later in addressing prelates and popes alike. In 1153 (–54?) in a letter to Pope Anastasius, for instance, we hear her telling the pope flatly that he is too old and tired to conduct his office properly and castigating him for banishing justice from his presence. The content of the letter to Bernard, read in isolation, gives the impression that, save for taking "a certain monk" into her confidence, Hildegard has kept absolute silence with regard to her visions and prophecies. She was, frankly, being quite disingenuous here, for as early as 1141, some five or six years before this letter to Bernard, she had already begun to compose her first major work, the *Scivias*. And, one might add, she had already received permission (nay, rather, command) from one of far greater authority than Bernard of Clairvaux to write and publish her message to the Christian world.

In the opening words of the *Scivias*, Hildegard describes a vision that she saw in the Living Light, and there she became aware of a mighty figure seated on a throne upon a great mountain, a figure so emanating with resplendent light that she could scarce see Him. And this figure, undoubtedly God Himself, cried out to her in a mighty voice, saying:

> O human creature, fragile dust of the earth and ashes of ashes, cry out, speak, and instruct the people about the entry of pure salvation into the world. Teach those people who, although they understand the inner meaning of the

Scripture, refuse to preach it because they are too lukewarm and sluggish to preserve God's justice. Open up to them the mysteries that they are too fearful to reveal, but instead conceal to no avail in a hidden field. Burst forth into a fountain of abundance and overflow them with mystical knowledge, until they, who now think you contemptible because of Eve's transgression, are overwhelmed by your mighty torrent. For you have received your insight into these profound matters not from human beings but from the lofty and mighty Judge on high.

Yet despite this injunction from heaven itself, Hildegard is quite aware that she must gain the favor of the ecclesiastical authorities before she will be able to publish her work, and in order to accomplish this she must show that she is not just some pride-filled woman, either deluded by the devil or out for her own gain in the world. Hence the deferential tone of her letter to Bernard with its stress on herself as the unwilling, as it were, recipient of the message from on high.

Letter 1 ❧ to Bernard of Clairvaux

O venerable father Bernard, I lay my claim before you, for, highly honored by God, you bring fear to the immoral foolishness of this world and, in your intense zeal and burning love for the Son of God, gather men into Christ's army to fight under the banner of the cross against pagan savagery.[2] I beseech you in the name of the Living God to give heed to my queries.

Father, I am greatly disturbed by a vision which has appeared to me through divine revelation, a vision seen not with my fleshly eyes but only in my spirit. Wretched, and indeed more than wretched in my womanly condition, I have from earliest childhood seen great

---

2. St. Bernard's was a leading voice in calling upon kings and knights to take up the cross in the Second Crusade.

marvels which my tongue has no power to express but which the Spirit of God has taught me that I may believe. Steadfast and gentle father, in your kindness respond to me, your unworthy servant, who has never, from her earliest childhood, lived one hour free from anxiety. In your piety and wisdom look in your spirit, as you have been taught by the Holy Spirit, and from your heart bring comfort to your handmaiden.

Through this vision which touches my heart and soul like a burning flame, teaching me profundities of meaning, I have an inward understanding of the Psalter, the Gospels, and other volumes. Nevertheless, I do not receive this knowledge in German. Indeed, I have no formal training at all, for I know how to read only on the most elementary level, certainly with no deep analysis.[3] But please give me your opinion in this matter, because I am untaught and untrained in exterior material, but am only taught inwardly, in my spirit. Hence my halting, unsure speech.

When I hear from your pious wisdom, I will be comforted. For with the single exception of a certain monk[4] in whose exemplary life I have the utmost confidence, I have not dared to tell these things to anyone, since there are so many heresies abroad in the land,[5] as I have heard. I have, in fact, revealed all my secrets to this man, and he has given me consolation, for these are great and fearsome matters.

---

3. Hildegard's point is not that she can scarcely read, but that she does not read like the scholars, laboring to extract the inner meaning from abstruse texts. Indeed, her learning, she maintains, does not come in this way at all, but from heaven itself. Her stress here, as throughout her life, is on the divine source of her understanding.

4. This was Volmar of St. Disibod, Hildegard's early teacher, who remained her confidant, secretary, and friend for many years, until his death in 1173.

5. The reference is to the various schismatic sects with which the twelfth century was rife. When Pope Eugenius III came into France in 1147, for example, he was shocked at the large number of heretics there, and, in fact, commissioned the recipient of this letter, Bernard, to deal with them.

Now, father, for the love of God, I seek consolation from you, that I may be assured. More than two years ago, indeed, I saw you in a vision, like a man looking straight into the sun, bold and unafraid. And I wept, because I myself am so timid and fearful. Good and gentle father, I have been placed in your care so that you might reveal to me through our correspondence whether I should speak these things openly or keep my silence, because I have great anxiety about this vision with respect to how much I should speak about what I have seen and heard. In the meantime, because I have kept silent about this vision, I have been laid low, bedridden in my infirmities, and am unable to raise myself up.

Therefore, I weep with sorrow before you. For in my nature, I am unstable because I am caught in the winepress,[6] that tree rooted in Adam by the devil's deceit which brought about his exile into this wayward world. Yet, now, rising up, I run to you. And I say to you: You are not inconstant, but are always lifting up the tree, a victor in your spirit, lifting up not only yourself but also the whole world unto salvation. You are indeed the eagle gazing directly at the sun.

And so I beseech your aid, through the serenity of the Father and through His wondrous Word and through the sweet moisture of compunction, the Spirit of truth [cf. John 14.17; 16.13], and through that holy sound, which all creation echoes, and through that same Word which gave birth to the world, and through the

---

6. Here is a striking example of Hildegard's sometimes intricately complex and interwoven imagery. This image seems to be a fusion of the tree of the garden of Eden and the winepress (where the grapes of wrath are trod) of Isaiah 63.3, already being used in the twelfth century as a figure of the crucifixion. Compare the following quotation from the *Scivias* (I.iii.31.623ff): "A bright light appeared for the assurance and salvation of mankind: the Son of God dressed himself in the poverty of a human body, and shining like a burning star in the midst of shadowy clouds, He was placed on the winepress where wine without the sediment of fermentation was to be pressed out. For the cornerstone itself fell on the winepress, and produced such wine that it gave forth the finest fragrance of sweetness."

sublimity of the Father, who sent the Word with sweet fruitfulness into the womb of the Virgin, from which He soaked up flesh, just as honey is surrounded by the honeycomb.[7] And may that Sound, the power of the Father, fall upon your heart and lift up your spirit so that you may respond expeditiously to these words of mine, taking care, of course, to seek all these things from God—with regard to the person or the mystery itself—while you are passing through the gateway of your soul, so that you may come to know all these things in God. Farewell, be strong in your spirit, and be a mighty warrior for God. Amen.

The following rather perfunctory response from Bernard, while not as warm as one might have expected as a reply to such a passionate plea, nevertheless fulfills Hildegard's wishes by acknowledging that her gift is from a divine source and rejoicing "in the grace of God which is in you." Although evidence is scanty, it seems that Bernard also intervened on Hildegard's behalf with Pope Eugenius, who just happened to be holding a synod at neighboring Trier. The pope then sent legates to Mount St. Rupert, whence they brought back the completed portion of the Scivias, *and the pope himself read it to the assembled cardinals and the archbishop. As a result, it was unanimously decided that Hildegard should be encouraged in her work.*

Letter 2 ❧ *from Bernard of Clairvaux*

Brother Bernard, called Abbot of Clairvaux, offers to Hildegard, beloved daughter in Christ, whatever the prayer of a sinner can accomplish.

---

7. The image of the womb of the Virgin as a honeycomb or beehive derives ultimately from the fanciful notion in the bestiaries of bees giving birth virginally. The idea is given full expression in the following stanza of an anonymous Latin poem preserved in a manuscript of the eleventh century: "No creature is like the bee/That bears the symbol of chastity/Except the One who bore the Christ/In her inviolate womb chastely."

It is perhaps to be attributed to your humility that you appear to have a higher regard for our poor abilities than I myself would admit. All the same, I have made some effort to respond to your letter of love, although the press of business forces me to respond more briefly than I would have liked.

We rejoice in the grace of God which is in you. And, further, we most earnestly urge and beseech you to recognize this gift as grace and to respond eagerly to it with all humility and devotion, with the knowledge that "God resisteth the proud, and giveth grace to the humble" [James 4.6; I Pet 5.5].[8] But, on the other hand, when the learning and the anointing (which reveals all things to you) are within, what advice could we possibly give?

And so we ask all the more, and humbly beseech, that you remember us before God, and not only us but also those who are bound to us in spiritual community.

In the meantime, Hildegard writes to the pope on her own behalf, seeking approval of her writing. Note her continuing emphasis on her feminine humility. Here too, for the first time, she makes use of her famous metaphor of herself as a small feather wafted aloft by the breath of God.

Letter 3   to Pope Eugenius III

O gentle father, poor little woman though I am, I have written those things to you which God saw fit to teach me in a true vision, by mystic inspiration.

O radiant father, through your representatives you have come to us, just as God foreordained, and you have seen some of the writings of truthful visions, which I received from the Living Light, and you have listened to these visions in the embraces of your heart.

---

8. This is a theme (with the same biblical verses being cited) that Hildegard is to hear again and again. The stress on humility is not, of course, unusual, but it seems particularly prominent in exhortations to Hildegard, because of the problem of gender.

A part of this writing has now been completed. But still that same Light has not left me, but it blazes in my soul, just as it has from my childhood. Therefore, I send this letter to you now, as God has instructed me. And my spirit desires that the Light of Light shine in you and purify your eyes and arouse your spirit to your duty concerning my writings, so that your soul may be crowned, which will be pleasing to God. In their instability, many people, those wise in worldly things, disparage these writings of mine, criticizing me, a poor creature formed from a rib, ignorant of philosophical matters.

Therefore, father of pilgrims, hear Him Who Is: A mighty king sat in his palace, surrounded by great columns girt with golden bands and beautifully adorned with many pearls and precious stones. It pleased this king to touch a small feather so that it flew miraculously, and a powerful wind sustained it so that it would not fall.

Now, He who is the Living Light shining in the heavens and in the abyss and Who lies hidden in the hearts of those who hear Him says again to you: Prepare this writing for the hearing of those who receive Me and make it fruitful with the juice of sweet savor; make it a root of the branches and a leaf flying in the face of the devil, and you will have eternal life. Do not spurn these mysteries of God, because they have a necessity which lies hidden and has not yet been revealed. May the odor be sweet in you and may you not grow weary on the strait way.

Criticism and Response

II

At this point, everything seems to be going well for Hildegard, exceedingly well. She has at last managed to break through her forty-year wall of silence, and she has, somehow, learned a way to finesse her male-dominated world so that she can sound forth—confidently, authoritatively—her divinely inspired message. She has, against all odds, gained the approval of the pope, accompanied by the encouragement to continue with her writing. She has written a large portion of her first major work describing, and interpreting, her visions, a work that she would bring to its final form in 1151. And even before completion of that work, her reputation having spread abroad, apparently by word of mouth, she has become widely recognized as prophet and seer. Things are going very well indeed.

But the strait way can be exceptionally rocky—even for saints. Very early on—sometime between 1148 and 1150—Hildegard received a severe letter of criticism, a missive masquerading, to be sure, as a mere inquiry into the unusual ceremonies practiced in her community,

23

but one quite acid in tone. Moreover, Hildegard's decision to move her company of nuns and establish her own monastery raised up surprisingly long-lasting animosity among the monks of her home monastery. And, most grievous of all, she was to be deprived of the companionship of her beloved assistant and friend. These difficulties and tensions can be observed in detail in the correspondence immediately following.

The following letter can only be described as a mordant personal attack on Hildegard couched in the smarmy language of religious piety. Sent out early in Hildegard's career (that is, her public career),[1] having been written sometime between the years 1148 and 1150, the letter is based entirely on report and rumor about Hildegard's peculiar practices in her community. For although Tengswich has heard that the seer is busily engaged in writing down the "secrets of heaven," revealed to her by "an angel," she has, herself, not seen any of these. Well written in a style suffused with irony that verges at times on sarcasm, the letter gives a graphic and deliciously detailed description of the goings-on, so offensive to Tengswich's pietistic tastes, in that, as she saw it, all-too-liberal community. Then, as now, there were those religious conservatives who have difficulty accepting any changes in the old-time religion. This letter is a very significant document for an understanding of Hildegard, for from no other source do we get such an elaborate description of her practices as head of her own community. It is quite remarkable too that these extraordinary ceremonies seem to have been taking place even before the removal to the more private community at Mount St. Rupert, for that move did not take place until 1150.

Letter 4 from Mistress Tengswich

To Hildegard, mistress of the brides of Christ, Tengswich, unworthy superior of the sisters at Andernach, with a prayer that she eventually be joined to the highest order of spirits in heaven.

---

1. It is important to make the distinction, for although Hildegard has not yet launched her public career through the completion of the *Scivias*, she has been in charge of her community of nuns since the death of Jutta in 1136.

CRITICISM AND RESPONSE

The report of your saintliness has flown far and wide and has brought to our attention things wondrous and remarkable. And, insignificant as we are, these reports have highly commended the loftiness of your outstanding and extraordinary mode of religious life to us. We have learned from a number of people that an angel from above reveals many secrets of heaven for you to record, difficult as they are for mortal minds to grasp, as well as some things that you are to do, not in accordance with human wisdom, but as God himself instructs them to be done.

We have, however, also heard about certain strange and irregular practices that you countenance. They say that on feast days your virgins stand in the church with unbound hair when singing the psalms and that as part of their dress they wear white, silk veils, so long that they touch the floor. Moreover, it is said that they wear crowns of gold filigree, into which are inserted crosses on both sides and the back, with a figure of the Lamb on the front, and that they adorn their fingers with golden rings. And all this despite the express prohibition of the great shepherd of the Church, who writes in admonition: Let women comport themselves with modesty "not with plaited hair, or gold, or pearls, or costly attire" [I Tim 2.9]. Moreover, that which seems no less strange to us is the fact that you admit into your community only those women from noble, well-established families and absolutely reject others who are of lower birth and of less wealth. Thus we are struck with wonder and are reeling in confusion when we ponder quietly in our heart that the Lord himself brought into the primitive Church humble fishermen and poor people, and that, later, at the conversion of the gentiles, the blessed Peter said: "In truth, I perceive that God is no respecter of persons" [Acts 10.34]. Nor should you be unmindful of the words of the Apostle in Corinthians: "Not many mighty, not many noble, but God hath chosen the contemptible and the ignoble things of this world" [I Cor 1.26–28]. We have examined as accurately as possible all the precedents laid down by the fathers of the Church,

to which all spiritual people must conform, and we have found nothing in them comparable to your actions.

O worthy bride of Christ, such unheard-of practices far exceed the capacity of our weak understanding, and strike us with no little wonder. And although we feeble little women wholeheartedly rejoice with all the esteem due your spiritual success, we still wish you to inform us on some points relative to this matter. Therefore, we have decided to send this humble little letter to you, saintly lady, asking by whose authority you can defend such practices, and we devoutly and meekly beseech, worthy lady, that you not disdain to write back to us as soon as possible. Farewell, and remember us in your prayers.

Hildegard's answer to the good mistress serves to substantiate Tengswich's detailed description of the unusual customs and ceremonies in her unusual community. Hildegard accepts everything; of no single detail does she suggest that it was merely the result of malicious rumor. Instead, she mounts an elaborate argument to justify her practices, and along the way produces what can only be called the highest paean of praise to womanhood that has come down to us from the Middle Ages, perhaps from any age. It is a splendid, scintillating piece of work.

Letter 5 *to Mistress Tengswich*

The Living Fountain says: Let a woman remain within her chamber so that she may preserve her modesty, for the serpent breathed the fiery danger of horrible lust into her. Why should she do this? Because the beauty of woman radiated and blazed forth in the primordial root, and in her was formed that chamber in which every creature lies hidden. Why is she so resplendent? For two reasons: on the one hand, because she was created by the finger of God and, on the other, because she was endowed with wondrous beauty. O, woman, what a splendid being you are! For you have set your foundation in the sun, and have conquered the world.

Paul the apostle, who flew to the heights but kept silent on earth so as not to reveal that which was hidden [cf. II Cor 12.4], observed that a woman who is subject to the power of her husband [cf. Ephes 5.22; Col 3.18], joined to him through the first rib, ought to preserve great modesty, by no means giving or displaying her vessel to another man who has no business with her, for that vessel belongs to her husband [cf. I Thess 4.4]. And let her do this in accordance with the word spoken by the master of the earth in scorn of the devil: "What God hath joined together, let no man put asunder" [Matt 19.6].

Listen: The earth keeps the grass green and vital, until winter conquers it. Then winter takes away the beauty of that flower, and the earth covers over its vital force so that it is unable to manifest itself as if it had never withered up, because winter has ravaged it. In a similar manner, a woman, once married, ought not to indulge herself in prideful adornment of hair or person, nor ought she to lift herself up to vanity, wearing a crown and other golden ornaments, except at her husband's pleasure, and even then with moderation.

But these strictures do not apply to a virgin, for she stands in the unsullied purity of paradise, lovely and unwithering, and she always remains in the full vitality of the budding rod. A virgin is not commanded to cover up her hair, but she willingly does so out of her great humility, for a person will naturally hide the beauty of her soul, lest, on account of her pride, the hawk carry it off.

Virgins are married with holiness in the Holy Spirit and in the bright dawn of virginity, and so it is proper that they come before the great High Priest as an oblation presented to God. Thus through the permission granted her and the revelation of the mystic inspiration of the finger of God, it is appropriate for a virgin to wear a white vestment, the lucent symbol of her betrothal to Christ, considering that her mind is made one with the interwoven whole, and keeping in mind the One to whom she is joined, as it is written: "Having his name, and the name of his Father, written on their foreheads" [Apoc 14.1] and also "These follow the Lamb whithersoever he goeth" [Apoc 14.4].

God also keeps a watchful eye on every person, so that a lower order will not gain ascendancy over a higher one, as Satan and the first man did, who wanted to fly higher than they had been placed. And who would gather all his livestock indiscriminately into one barn—the cattle, the asses, the sheep, the kids? Thus it is clear that differentiation must be maintained in these matters, lest people of varying status, herded all together, be dispersed through the pride of their elevation, on the one hand, or the disgrace of their decline, on the other, and especially lest the nobility of their character be torn asunder when they slaughter one another out of hatred. Such destruction naturally results when the higher order falls upon the lower, and the lower rises above the higher. For God establishes ranks on earth, just as in heaven with angels, archangels, thrones, dominions, cherubim, and seraphim. And they are all loved by God, although they are not equal in rank. Pride loves princes and nobles because of their illusions of grandeur, but hates them when they destroy that illusion. And it is written that "God does not cast off the mighty, since He himself is mighty" [Job 36.5]. He does not love people for their rank but for their works which derive their savor from Him, just as the Son of God says: "My food is to do the will" of my Father [John 4.34]. Where humility is found, there Christ always prepares a banquet. Thus when individuals seek after empty honor rather than humility, because they believe that one is preferable to the other, it is necessary that they be assigned to their proper place. Let the sick sheep be cast out of the fold, lest it infect the entire flock.

God has infused human beings with good understanding so that their name will not be destroyed. It is not good for people to grab hold of a mountain which they cannot possibly move. Rather, they should stand in the valley, gradually learning what they are capable of.

These words do not come from a human being but from the Living Light. Let the one who hears see and believe where these words come from.

In the year 1150 Hildegard suddenly announced that she had been instructed by God to remove herself and her nuns from their present location and to establish a new home, some thirty kilometers distant, in a place to be called Mount St. Rupert. From the moment of Hildegard's pronouncement, the move was vehemently opposed by the monks of St. Disibod. The opposition was fierce and acrimonious, and the abbot absolutely refused to grant permission for the move. One can easily understand the motives behind the monks' recalcitrance: Was this not the protégée whom they had nourished and protected since early childhood? Was this (female) person grown so prideful as to resist the (male) hierarchical rule established by God Himself? Or to express it in more selfish terms, Was this person to be allowed to leave, taking with her the fame and fortune she had achieved under their patronage? And, besides, Was there not the matter of the dowries of the noble young ladies who had become nuns in their community?

Hildegard eventually won out, but only by taking to her sickbed, as she often did in spiritual crises. By God's will, she lay rigid and inert in her bed. When the abbot of St. Disibod visited her in her sickroom and found that even by exerting all his strength, he could not, by any means, move her, he at last understood that all this was done by the will of the Lord, and he granted permission for the move. Hildegard was also assisted in legal affairs, the acquisition of the property, etc., by a local noblewoman, the Margravine Richardis von Stade, mother of one of her nuns, and by Heinrich, Archbishop of the diocese.

But the monks of Mount St. Disibod never quite forgave her for her singular act of independence. The following letters attest to that disapproval.

Here, Hildegard herself attests to the hostility of the monks of St. Disibod, at least from those who adamantly opposed her move and refused to forgive her "desertion." In this brief letter to the abbot, written probably in 1155, she describes the harsh treatment she received from the monks on her return to negotiate property rights.

Letter 6 🙠 to the Abbot of Mount St. Disibod

O you who are a father in your office—and how happy I am to say it—I pray that now you may be father to me in deed. I returned to the place where God has bequeathed to you the rod of his authority. But a mob of some of your monks rose up and gnashed their teeth at me, as if I were a bird of gloom or a horrid beast, and they bent their bows against me in order to drive me away. But I know for a fact that God moved me from that place for His own inscrutable purposes, for my soul was so agitated by His words and miracles that I believe I would have died before my time if I had remained there.

Now, salvation and blessing upon those who received me there with devotion; as for those others who wagged their heads at me [Lam 2.15], may God extend His grace to them, as He sees fit in His mercy.

Alas, O my mother,[2] with what sorrow and grief you have received me.

This letter was written sometime between 1150 and 1155, that is, within a few years (perhaps even a few months) after Hildegard's removal from Mount St. Disibod. The letter expresses very well the monks' dismay at their loss, and although this monk professes his acceptance of God's will in the matter, one wonders on reading his "we cannot fathom why God did this" whether he does not still question Hildegard's interpretation of that command.

Letter 7 🙠 from Adelbert, Prior at Mount St. Disibod

To Hildegard, truly filled with the grace of the Holy Spirit, Adelbert, monk (though unworthy) and prior at Mount St. Disibod, along

---

2. That is, the monastery at St. Disibod.

with the brothers of that same monastery, sends our prayers that you may ascend from virtue unto virtue and may see the God of gods in Zion [cf. Ps 83.8].

Since you send the words of your admonition into foreign regions and cause large numbers of people to desire the paths of righteousness, we (who have known you almost from the cradle and with whom you lived for many years) wonder why you have withdrawn the words of your celestial visions from us who thirst for them.

We remember how you were educated among us, how you were taught, how you were established in the religious life. For your instruction was that appropriate only to a woman, and a simple psalter was your only schoolbook. Yet without complaint you embraced the good and holy religious life. But the will of God filled you with celestial dew [cf. Gen 27.28] and opened up to you the magnitude of its secrets. And just as we were set to rejoice in these things with you, God took you away from us against our will, and gave you to other people. We cannot fathom why God did this, but, willy-nilly, we are suffering great distress from the deed. For we had hoped that the salvation of our monastery rested with you, but God disposed matters differently than we wished. Now, however, since we cannot stand against the will of God, we have yielded to it and rejoice with you, for through divine revelation you make many things clear that were, before, unseen and unheard, and you open doors that were closed before. Indeed, filled, as you are, with the Holy Spirit, you write many things which you never learned from man, things that holy and learned men marvel at.

Wherefore, although we are far from holy (because we remain sinners), we beseech you, both for the glory of God and for old and true fellowship, to remember us and to offer us some words of consolation. We ask also that you seek God's help for us, so that that which is least in us God may deign to supplement through the merits of your prayers. Farewell.

How long, O Lord, how long? as Hildegard might say. This letter, written "about 1170" (according to the standard edition) is vivid testimony of the continuing difficulties between the two institutions some twenty years after Hildegard's removal from Mount St. Disibod. It is clear that Hildegard is still exercised over the hostility of the monks of St. Disibod, and this letter to the abbot is harsh and shrill in its criticism.

Letter 8   to Helengerus, Abbot of Mount St. Disibod

In a spiritual vision which I received from God, I heard these words: If, amidst his desires, a man wishes to find his soul, he must abandon the wicked works of the flesh and affirm that God-given knowledge of the way to conduct his life. And so let his soul be the lady and his flesh his handmaiden, as the Psalmist says: "Blessed is the man whom thou shalt instruct, O Lord: and shalt teach him out of thy law" [Ps 93.12]. And who is this man? Why, he is the one who keeps his body under control like his handmaiden, and cherishes his soul as the lady he loves and serves. For the person who is impiously ferocious like a bear, but then renounces that ferocity and sighs in his soul for the loyal and merciful Sun of justice [cf. Mal 4.2]—that one pleases God. And God gives him charge over His precepts, placing in his hands an iron rod [cf. Ps 2.9] to teach his sheep the way to the mountain of myrrh [cf. Cant 4.6].

Now, listen and learn so that in the inwardness of your soul you will be ashamed. Sometimes you are like a bear which growls under its breath; but sometimes like an ass, not prudent in your duties, but, rather, worn down. Indeed, in some matters you are altogether useless, so that, in your impiety, you do not even put the malice of the bear into practice. You are also like certain kinds of birds, which do not fly on the heights and yet do not hug the earth, neither excelling nor being subject to harm.

The great Father of the household responds to character of this kind: "Ah, I do not like the shiftiness of your character, with your

CRITICISM AND RESPONSE

mind growling at my justice and failing to seek the proper solution from it, nursing instead a kind of growling inside yourself, like the growling of a bear. But when you do get a flash of insight, you pray for a little while, and then you grow weary again, and you do not even bother to finish your prayer, but you take the road which your body knows well, and you never fully renounce it. But sometimes your desires rise up to Me concerning some aspect which is not wholly sanctified by works, but resting only on your general acceptance of the faith. I sometimes have chosen people of unstable disposition like you so that I might hear the sound of their intellect, that is, what they were thinking to themselves. But when they were found to be of no use, they also fell." Therefore, do not let your mind despise the work which God does, for you do not know when He will strike you with His sword.

Poor little woman that I am, I see a black fire in you kindled against us, but use your good knowledge to consign it to oblivion, lest the grace and blessing of God depart from you during your time in office. Therefore, love the justice of God so that you may be loved by God, and faithfully trust in His miracles so that you may receive the eternal rewards.

If this letter is in answer to Hildegard's just above or, at least, after it—the editor simply dates both as "about 1170"—perhaps Hildegard finally got through to them. In any case, Helengerus, here, is clearly attempting to make peace between the two institutions. This dissension between the two monasteries has, after all, been going on for some twenty years at this point, for, it will be recalled that Hildegard made her move as early as 1150.

Letter 9 ຄ *from Helengerus, Abbot of Mount St. Disibod*

Helengerus, by the grace of God servant on Mount St. Disibod and overseer, though unworthy, of the Lord's flock there, along with the whole congregation of brothers, sends greetings to the venerable mother, Lady Hildegard of St. Rupert, who is fully illumined by the ray of divine splendor beyond all human understanding, as we know very well. May you abound in the gifts of the septiform Holy Spirit [cf. Apoc 3.1], and may you offer the cup of the holy fountain to the thirsty, so that you may receive your reward in heaven.

We know, beloved mother, that you recently came to us at the prompting, and indeed at the command, of the Paraclete, the holy spirit of Almighty God, "who wishes all men to be saved and to come to the knowledge of the truth" [I Tim 2.4]. And thus we offer our ceaseless, though unworthy, thanks to that Paraclete as best we can, because, to confess the truth, we have become fully aware of the burning power and strength of His illumination among us and indeed within us. At the same time we have, with one accord, cast off the inveterate hostility and animosity that we have nurtured for many years now, and we have come together fully into the unity of genuine divine love, as with one body and one spirit.

With earnest prayers we knock at the gate of your love, saintly lady, beseeching that you look to that brightness conferred upon you by divine grace and reveal to us whether, in fact, we are united in true love, which is the beginning of all good things, or if some root of dissension still lies unseen between us. For it is through this brightness that things concealed are disclosed to your love and things hidden from all other mortals are opened up to the eyes of your heart. Indeed, this is something you owe us as a debt, because you (along with your sisters) are the one who left us, admittedly not in spirit but only in body as we hope, and, indeed, know in truth. But with these minor matters out of the way—which, after all, we have already confessed—may we now request that you reveal to us in writing all the other, more important matters which you know to be contrary to the eyes of divine majesty.

CRITICISM AND RESPONSE

In this regard, all of us in full unanimity pound upon the gate of your love, beseeching you earnestly, fervently, for a written account of the deeds, virtues, and life of our patron, the blessed Disibod[3]—and not only ours, of course, but yours, for you were nourished under his roof from your earliest years. And we earnestly urge you, pious lady, and, with unwearying prayers poured forth, desire that you make known to us whatever God reveals to you about him, so that the memory of your own blessedness may be preserved through this record in praise of this our father.

May the almighty Father of eternal compassion inflame your devout mind with His radiant light, and may He offer to those who so sincerely desire it the cup that rekindles to life.

In this late letter, written probably in 1170, Hildegard reminisces about her return to Mount St. Disibod to negotiate for the property rights that she felt properly belonged to her own community. In no uncertain terms, Hildegard castigates the monks for their recalcitrant attitude and continuing animosity. It is true, however, that the portion of the letter that contains the bitterest denunciation (from "And according to the true vision" to "possession of my daughters' endowments") does not occur in all manuscripts and, therefore, may be spurious, but it does bear the very tone of Hildegard, and evidence from other sources attests the monks' hostility. Then unexpectedly and rather oddly in such a letter, Hildegard moves into a contemplation of her own death and the subsequent grief of her nuns at such an event.

Letter 10 ❧ to Her Own Community

O daughters, you who have followed in Christ's footsteps [cf. I Pet 2.21] in your love for chastity, and who have chosen me, poor little woman that I am, as a mother for yourselves—a choice made

---

3. Hildegard did indeed respond to this request by writing a life of St. Disibod.

in the humility of obedience in order to exalt God—I say these things not on my own accord but according to a divine revelation speaking through my motherly affection for you. I have found this monastery—this resting place of the relics of St. Rupert the confessor, to whose refuge you have fled—resplendent with miracles, by God's will, offering up a sacrifice of praise [cf. Ps 49.14]. I came to this place with the permission of my superiors and with God's assistance I gladly made it a home for myself and my followers.

Later, however, at God's admonition I paid a visit to Mount St. Disibod (which I had left with permission), where I presented the following petition to all who dwelt there: I requested that our monastery, as well as the alms accruing therefrom, be free and clear from their jurisdiction, for the sake of the salvation of our souls and our concern for the strict observance of the Rule. And according to the true vision I received, I said this to the father, that is, the abbot, of that monastery: The Serene Light says: "You should be a father to this community for the salvation of the souls of My daughters abiding in My mystic planting. The alms bestowed upon them have nothing to do with you or your brothers, but your monastery should be a place of sanctuary for them. But if it is your will to persevere in gnashing your teeth at us with your verbal assaults, then you will be like the Amalekites [cf. I Sam 30.1f] and like Antiochus, who, as it is written, stripped the temple of the Lord bare [cf. I Macch 1.23f; 6.12]. But if any among you say to yourselves maliciously: We intend to diminish their holdings—then 'I Who Am' [Ex 3.14] say that you are the worst sort of despoilers. If you attempt to take from them the shepherd who applies spiritual medicine,[4] then again I say to you that you are like the sons of Belial [cf. I Sam 2.12; 10.27], and that in this matter you are not considering the

---

4. That is, the provost and spiritual adviser, Volmar.

justice of God, and, for this reason, the justice of God will destroy you."[5] And when with these words, I, a poor little form of a woman, sought from that abbot and his brothers the autonomy of our monastery and the unencumbered possession of my daughters' endowments, they granted me this freedom and even promised me a written charter. Everyone—from the highest to the lowest—who saw, heard, and perceived these things displayed the greatest benevolence regarding these matters so that they were confirmed in writing, in accordance with God's will. Let all who cling to God heed and learn this and affirm this matter with good will, and perfect it and stand by it so that they may receive the same blessing that God gave Jacob and Israel [cf. Gen 32.26ff].

O how loudly these daughters of mine will lament when their mother dies, for they will no longer suckle her breasts. And so for a long time with groans and wails and tears they will say: Alas, alas! Gladly would we suck our mother's breasts if we but had her here with us now! Therefore, O daughters of God, I admonish you to love one another, just as from my youth I, your mother, have admonished you, so that in this good will you might be a bright light with the angels, and strong in your spirits, just as Benedict, your father, instructed you. May the Holy Spirit send you His gifts, because after my death you will no longer hear my voice. But never forget the sound of my voice among you, for it has so often resounded in love among you.

Now, my daughters are grieved in their hearts out of the sadness they feel for their mother, and they sigh and look to heaven. Later, they will shine with a bright, radiant light through the grace of God, and they will become valiant warriors in God's house. Therefore, if

---

5. Clearly, the quotation begins and ends as indicated, but note how in the third sentence of the quotation, Hildegard shifts into "us," where "them," as in the preceding sentence, might have been expected. This kind of shifting between the voice of the Living Light and Hildegard's own voice is not uncommon in her writing.

any one of my daughters seeks to cause discord and dissension in the spiritual discipline of this monastery, may the gift of the Holy Spirit root this desire out of her heart. Yet if she should do this out of total contempt for God, may the hand of the Lord strike her down in the presence of all the people, for such a one has deserved to be confounded.

Therefore, O my daughters, dwell in this place with all devotion and steadfastness, for you have chosen it as a place in which to serve in the army of God [cf. II Tim 2.4]. Do this so that, in Him, you may receive the rewards of Heaven.

Richardis von Stade

In 1151, soon after (or immediately before) the completion of the *Scivias*, Hildegard experienced the greatest personal loss of her life. It was a terrible blow, coming, as it did, suddenly and, apparently, unexpectedly from a totally unanticipated source. Richardis von Stade, Hildegard's close companion and assistant in producing her first major work, her beloved friend and the person she loved, as she says in a later letter, "in every aspect of your life," had been elected abbess to another monastery in a distant diocese and was soon to leave to take up her duties there. It may have been that Richardis had grown weary of her position as subordinate nun and had herself actively sought this elevation in the hierarchy of the Church, or it may have been, as Hildegard seems to think, that she was the passive object of her mother's or her brother's ambition for her. Whatever the truth of the matter, Hildegard felt betrayed and deserted by this sudden reversal of fortune, and Hildegard was not one to sit supinely by when she felt a course of action was inherently wrong and out of concordance with God's eternal plan. Therefore, she swung into action immediately, firing off missive after missive, alternately pleading, wheedling, threatening, stubbornly refusing to the end to give in to the inevitable. Letters poured out from Mount St. Rupert—to the mother, to the brother, to the archbishop who had ordered her to comply, and, ultimately, to the pope himself. Clearly, Hildegard was not disposed to give up without a fight, and it seems clear that she thought (in vain, as it turned out) that she could win. Fortunately, we can follow this tumultuous controversy pretty much in its entirety, for the correspondence (with the unhappy exception of Hildegard's letter to the pope) has been preserved. On reading the following letters, it should be borne well in mind that this event took place very early on in Hildegard's career, long before she became the established prophet and seer of her later years, revered, as it were, by all of Christendom.

The following letter to the Margravine[1] Richardis von Stade, mother of the nun Richardis, is the first volley in Hildegard's battle to nullify the election and keep her beloved companion by her side. Up until this point, the Margravine had been Hildegard's firm ally, staunchly supporting her, for instance, in her decision to leave her home monastery and establish her own institution at Mount St. Rupert. Therefore, Hildegard must have felt that she had some little sway with her correspondent, even though she probably suspected that the mother was the prime mover behind this political decision to elevate her daughter. The letter is a purely personal, anguished plea, for Hildegard does not here adopt the voice of her divine authority as she does in later letters on the subject. Nevertheless, she minces no words, with her reiterated "certainly, certainly, certainly not God's will." Considering the final outcome of the matter, the letter is a starkly prescient denunciation, and one can easily imagine the mother remembering those last terrible sentences in her grief and remorse "with bitter groans and tears."

---

1. The wife or widow of a Margrave, the military governor of a German border province.

RICHARDIS VON STADE

Letter 11 🙢 *to the Margravine Richardis von Stade*

I beseech and urge you not to trouble my soul so grievously that you make me weep bitter tears, and not to lacerate my heart with terrible wounds on account of my most beloved daughters Richardis and Adelheid.[2] I see them now glowing in the dawn and ornamented with pearls of virtues. Beware, lest by your will, advice, and support, their senses and souls are deprived of that high state of honor. For this position of abbess that you desire for them is certainly, certainly, certainly not God's will, nor compatible with the salvation of their souls. Therefore, if you are the mother of these your daughters, beware not to become the ruin of their souls, for, afterward, although you would not wish it, you would grieve with bitter groans and tears. May God illuminate and strengthen your sense and your soul in this brief time you have to live.

Addressing the problem of Hildegard's reluctance to release the nun Richardis, this letter from the archbishop of her diocese issues a direct, unambivalent order to Hildegard. As the letter makes clear, Heinrich understands the character of his subordinate very well indeed and is, therefore, quite vehement in his command, giving notice imperatively that a negative response will simply not do.

Letter 12 🙢 *from Heinrich, Archbishop of Mainz*

Heinrich, archbishop of the see of Mainz by the grace of God, sends his grace with fatherly affection to Hildegard, beloved mistress of the community at Mount St. Rupert the Confessor.

    Although we have heard of your many wonderful miracles, we have been slothful, we know, by not visiting you as often as we could. But burdened as we are by so much business, we are

---

2. Adelheid, who was also leaving to serve as abbess in a different community, was the Margravine's granddaughter.

sometimes scarcely able to lift our heart to those things which are eternal, and we do it slowly at that. But to come to the point, we hereby inform you that some messengers, monks of a certain noble church have come in petition to us with respect to a sister who is a nun in your monastery. They earnestly request that this sister be given up to them, since she has been duly elected abbess. Thus by the authority of our position as prelate and father, we give you this command and, in commanding, enjoin you to release this sister immediately to those who seek and desire her. If you accede to these requests, you will know our gratitude from now on in even greater measure than you have known it so far; but if not, we will issue the same command to you again in even stronger terms, and we will not leave off until you fulfill our commands in this matter.

Speaking through the voice of the Living Light, Hildegard responds to the archbishop, and, supported by that divine authority, she utterly rejects his command. Indeed, she goes on the offense and accuses him of the sin of simony, the sale of Church offices for monetary gain. The tone of this letter, different in kind from that addressed to the Margravine, is harsh and imperious.

Letter 13 to Heinrich, Archbishop of Mainz

The Bright Fountain, truthful and just, says, "These legal pretexts brought forward to establish authority over this girl have no weight in God's eyes, for I—high, deep, all-encompassing, a descending light—neither initiated nor wanted them. Rather, they have been manufactured in the conniving audacity of ignorant hearts. Let all the faithful hear these things with the open ears of their hearts, and not with the outward ears, like a beast which hears the sound, but not the meaning of a single word. The Spirit of God says earnestly: 'O shepherds, wail and mourn over the present time, because you do not know what you are doing when you sweep aside the duties established by God in favor of opportunities for money and the foolishness of wicked men who do not fear God.'"

And so your malicious curses and threatening words are not to be obeyed. You have raised up your rods of punishment arrogantly, not to serve God, but to gratify your own perverted will.

This letter was sent out to Richardis's brother, who was archbishop over the diocese where Richardis was assigned. By this time Richardis has already been installed in her new position, for Hildegard pleads for her restoration to Mount St. Rupert. Once again, as with the Margravine, Hildegard speaks in her own voice, although she continues to insist that it is God's will that she speaks. And, once again, she raises the specter of simony, perhaps not the most politically expedient move to make in this instance.

Letter 14 ❦ *to Hartwig, Archbishop of Bremen*

You are a man worthy of great praise, as one must be who holds the episcopal office in direct succession from almighty God Himself. Therefore, may your eye see God, your intellect grasp His justice, and your heart burn brightly in the love of God, so that your spirit may not grow weak. Be zealous to build the tower of celestial Jerusalem, and may God give you that sweetest mother Mercy as your assistant. Be a bright star shining in the darkness of the night of wicked men, and be a swift hart running to the fountain of living water [cf. John 4.10]. Be alert, for many shepherds are blind and halt nowadays, and they are seizing the lucre of death, choking out God's justice.

O dear man, your soul is dearer to me than your family.[3] Now hear me, cast down as I am, miserably weeping at your feet. My

---

3. Despite one's first impression, this remark is not apparently an invidious one, that is, that he is dearer to her than his family since they have already turned down her request. It is rather an attempt to put the case on the proper footing: that spiritual matters take precedence over familial influence and power, which is her whole argument here. Our thanks to Barbara Newman for her assistance in helping us understand the point being made.

spirit is exceedingly sad, because a certain horrible man[4] has trampled underfoot my desire and will (and not mine alone, but also my sisters' and friends'), and has rashly dragged our beloved daughter Richardis out of our cloister. Since God knows all things, He knows where pastoral care is useful, and so let no person of faith canvass for such an office. Thus if anyone, in his madness, willfully seeks to gain ecclesiastic office, he is a rapacious wolf seeking the delights of power more than the will of God. The soul of such a person, therefore, never seeks spiritual office with proper faith. Therein lies simony.

It was, therefore, inappropriate for our abbot, in his blindness and ignorance, to involve this holy soul in this affair and, in the blindness of his spirit, to encourage such great temerity. If our daughter had remained content, God would have fulfilled his glorious purpose for her.

I do not oppose any selection God has made, nor would I ever do so. Therefore, in the name of Him who gave His life for you and in the name of his holy Mother, I beseech you, you who hold the episcopal office in the order of Melchisedech [cf. Ps 109.4], to send my dearest daughter back to me.[5] If you do so, God will give you the blessing which Isaac gave to his son Jacob [cf. Gen 27.27–29] and which He gave through his angel to Abraham for his obedience [cf. Gen 22.15–18].

Hear me now, and do not cast off my words, as your mother, your sister, and Count Hermann have all done. I am doing you no harm not consonant with the will of God and the salvation of your sister's soul, but I seek to be consoled through her and her through me. What God has ordained, I do not oppose.

---

4. Hildegard is speaking of Kuno, abbot of St. Disibod, for whom she has little affection in any case, since, among other things, he had attempted to prevent her move to Mount St. Rupert.

5. Bassum, the monastery where Richardis had taken up her duties, lay in Hartwig's diocese, and thus he would indeed have had the authority to return her.

RICHARDIS VON STADE

May God grant you the blessing of the dew of heaven [cf. Gen 27.28], and may all the choirs of angels bless you if you listen to me, God's servant, and if you fulfill God's will in this matter.

This letter from the pope is in response to a letter from Hildegard, a letter which, most unfortunately, has not come down to us. In a final, desperate effort to retrieve Richardis, Hildegard fired off a letter to this court of last resort, a really quite audacious act on her part, but one which sharply underlines her sense of the righteousness of her cause. Eugenius's response, however, is, in effect, a denial of Hildegard's request, for he simply throws the matter back in the lap of Heinrich, Archbishop of Mainz, who had already made his stance clear. The proviso that he gives for the return of Richardis was a mere matter of form, a face-saving device on the part of the pope, since the monastery to which Richardis was assigned was firmly established in observance of the Benedictine Rule. Eugenius opens his letter with high praise for Hildegard, and it is notable how fully established Hildegard's reputation as prophet and seer has become even at this early stage in her career.

Letter 15 from Pope Eugenius III

Bishop Eugenius, servant of the servants of God, to Hildegard, beloved daughter in Christ, mistress of Mount St. Rupert, greetings and apostolic blessing.

We rejoice, my daughter, and we exult in the Lord, because your honorable reputation has spread so far and wide that many people regard you as "the odour of life unto life" [II Cor 2.16], and the multitudes of the faithful cry out, "Who is she that goeth up by the desert, as a pillar of smoke of aromatical spices?" [Cant 3.6]. Therefore, since it is clear to us that, up to this present time, your soul has been so kindled by the fire of divine love that you have no need of any exhortation to perform good works, we consider it superfluous to exhort you further or with a prop of words attempt to support a spirit which already sufficiently rests on divine virtue.

All the same, because a fire is increased by the bellows and a swift horse is impelled to greater speed by the spurs, we feel it

45

incumbent upon us to remind you that the palm of glory belongs not to the one who begins but to the one who finishes the race, as the Lord says, "To him, that overcometh, I will give to eat of the tree of life, which is" in the middle of paradise [Apoc 2.7]. And so bear in mind, my daughter, that the ancient serpent who cast the first man out of Paradise longs to destroy the great (like Job) and, having consumed Judas, seeks power to sift the apostles [cf. Luke 22.31]. Moreover, as you know, many are called but few chosen [cf. Matt 22.14], so bring yourself into that small number and persist all the way to the end in your holy calling, and instruct the sisters entrusted to your care in the works of salvation so that, with them, you may be able with the help of the Lord to come to that joy "that eye hath not seen, nor ear heard, neither hath it entered into the heart of man" [I Cor 2.9].

Finally, we have delegated that matter you wished to consult us about to our brother Heinrich, archbishop of Mainz. His task will be to make sure that the Rule is strictly observed in that monastery entrusted to that sister (the nun that you delivered up to him)—either that or to send her back to your supervision. The transcript of my letter to him will give you the details.

This poignant, heart-rending letter is Hildegard's final acceptance of that which she cannot change. One cannot grasp the full emotional content of this letter without recognizing the Biblical language and imagery that Hildegard employs to express the depth of her feeling. "Why have you forsaken me," she cries out in her grief, echoing the words of Christ in His Passion, just as her later lament ("Now, let all who have grief like mine mourn with me") would have inevitably recalled the words of the liturgy for Good Friday. There is a stark, unresolved tension here between divine and human love, as Hildegard seeks desperately to understand her woeful emotional turmoil in conventional Christian terms. In the opening of the letter she seeks to use her thwarted love for Richardis as a lesson to herself as a sinning human being not to put her trust in transitory earthly things—not even the love of one human being for another—but to turn her eyes to the supernal, everlasting love, which never deserts or fails. And, then, just as she has resolved her dilemma and applied the balm of this lesson to her heart, the dam of pent-up emotion bursts: "Why hast thou forsaken me," and "let all who have grief like mine mourn with me!" In the letter Hildegard addresses Richardis as both "daughter" (the nun under her tutelage) and "mother" (since Richardis is now abbess in a monastery superior to her own), and refers to herself as an "orphan," once again recalling the words of Christ to His disciples, "I will not leave you orphans, I will come to you" (John 14.18). This lovely, touching letter would have been a fitting end to the conflict, but there are more, and more grievous, things to come.

Letter 16 ❧ *to Richardis*

Daughter, listen to me, your mother, speaking to you in the spirit: my grief flies up to heaven. My sorrow is destroying the great confidence and consolation that I once had in mankind. From now on I will say: "It is good to trust in the Lord, rather than to trust in princes" [Ps 117.9]. The point of this Scripture is that a person ought to look to the living height, with vision unobstructed by earthly love and feeble faith, which the airy humor of earth renders transient and short-lived. Thus a person looking at God directs his sight to the sun like an eagle. And for this reason one should not depend on a person of high birth, for such a one inevitably withers like a flower. This was the very transgression I myself committed because of my love for a certain noble individual.

Now I say to you: As often as I sinned in this way, God revealed that sin to me, either through some sort of difficulty or some kind of grief, just as He has now done regarding you, as you well know.

Now, again I say: Woe is me, mother, woe is me, daughter, "Why have you forsaken me" [Ps 21.2; Matt 27.46; Mark 15.34] like an orphan? I so loved the nobility of your character, your wisdom, your chastity, your spirit, and indeed every aspect of your life that many people have said to me: What are you doing?

Now, let all who have grief like mine mourn with me, all who, in the love of God, have had such great love in their hearts and minds for a person—as I had for you—but who was snatched away from them in an instant, as you were from me. But, all the same, may the angel of God go before you, may the Son of God protect you, and may his mother watch over you. Be mindful of your poor desolate mother, Hildegard, so that your happiness may not fade.

Suddenly, unexpectedly (for she was only 28 or so), Richardis has died, and this letter from her brother Hartwig was sent to Hildegard to inform her of the sad event. The main purpose of the letter is, of course, to fulfill the Christian duty of informing Hildegard that Richardis made a good Christian end, confessing the Trinity and Unity of God, etc., but he does, at least in an oblique way, accept some little blame in the preceding affair with his "if I have any right to ask" and with his reference to the fault "which indeed was mine, not hers." He also seeks to lighten the blow to Hildegard by informing her of Richardis's longing for her former cloister and her intention to return for a visit if death had not intervened.

Letter 17 ❧ *from Hartwig, Archbishop of Bremen*

Hartwig, archbishop of Bremen, brother of the abbess Richardis, sends that which is in the place of a sister and more than a sister, obedience, to Hildegard, mistress of the sisters of St. Rupert.

I write to inform you that our sister—my sister in body, but yours in spirit—has gone the way of all flesh, little esteeming that honor I bestowed upon her. And (while I was on my way to see the earthly king) she was obedient to her lord, the heavenly King. I am happy to report that she made her last confession in a saintly and pious way and that after her confession she was anointed with consecrated oil. Moreover, filled with her usual Christian spirit, she tearfully expressed her longing for your cloister with her whole heart. She then committed herself to the Lord through His mother and St. John. And sealed three times with the sign of the cross, she confessed the Trinity and Unity of God, and died on October 29 in perfect faith, hope, and charity [cf. I Cor 13.13], as we know for certain. Thus I ask as earnestly as I can, if I have any right to ask, that you love her as much as she loved you, and if she appeared to have any fault—which indeed was mine, not hers—at least have regard for the tears that she shed for your cloister, which many witnessed. And if death had not prevented, she would have come to you as soon as she was able to get permission. But since death did intervene, be assured that, God willing, I will come in her place. May God, who repays all good deeds, recompense you fully in this world and in the future for all the good things you did for her, you alone, more even than relatives or friends; may He repay that benevolence of yours which she rejoiced in before God and me. Please convey my thanks to your sisters for all their kindness.

If there were ever a time when an "I-told-you-so" response might have been appropriate, this was it. Yet Hildegard is magnanimous and considerate in her answer to Hartwig, totally respectful of his grief, and hers. And although she mentions the grief he had caused her, she does so only to inform him that she has cast it completely out of her heart. Nothing in the correspondence displays the magnificence of this gracious lady better than this brief letter.

Letter 18 ❧ to Hartwig, Archbishop of Bremen

O how great a miracle there is in the salvation of those souls so looked upon by God that His glory has no hint of shadow in them. But He works in them like a mighty warrior who takes care not to be defeated by anyone, so that his victory may be sure.

Just so, dear man, was it with my daughter Richardis, whom I call both daughter and mother, because I cherished her with divine love, as indeed the Living Light had instructed me to do in a very vivid vision.

God favored her so greatly that worldly desire had no power to embrace her. For she always fought against it, even though she was like a flower in her beauty and loveliness in the symphony of this world. While she was still living in the body, in fact, I heard the following words concerning her in a true vision: "O virginity, you are standing in the royal bridal chamber." Now, in the tender shoot of virginity, she has been made a part of that most holy order, and the daughters of Zion rejoice [Zach 2.10, 9.9]. But the ancient serpent had attempted to deprive her of that blessed honor by assaulting her through her human nobility. Yet the mighty Judge drew this my daughter to Himself, cutting her off from all human glory. Therefore, although the world loved her physical beauty and her worldly wisdom while she was still alive, my soul has the greatest confidence in her salvation. For God loved her more. Therefore, He was unwilling to give His beloved to a heartless lover, that is, to the world.[6]

Now you, dear Hartwig, you who sit as Christ's representative, fulfill the desire of your sister's soul, as obedience demands. And just as she always had your interests at heart, so you now take thought for her soul, and do good works as she wished. Now, as for me, I cast out of my heart that grief you caused me in the matter of this my daughter. May God grant you, through the prayers of the saints, the dew of His grace and reward in the world to come.

This letter is from Adelheid, that other nun for whom (along with Richardis) Hildegard petitioned the Margravine. The year when the letter was written is unknown; the standard edition of the letters gives a twenty-year time frame for its composition. At all events, it was written sometime after the death of

---

6. The blending of secular and divine love in this paragraph, or, perhaps better, the expression of divine love in earthly terms is simply exquisite: the beautiful, highborn lady, beloved for both her beauty and her wit and wooed by two very different lovers, is carried off by the worthiest of the two.

Richardis, and perhaps a long time thereafter. Adelheid recalls her early years under Hildegard's care and tutelage with great fondness and seeks the honor of her prayers for herself and her community. Hildegard had also written a couple of letters to Adelheid, but since they were simply letters of general advice and admonition (also with no specific date of composition), they have no place in this anthology of personal correspondence.

Letter 19   from the Abbess Adelheid

Adelheid, unworthy abbess of the church at Gandersheim, to Hildegard, beloved mother of Mount St. Rupert, with a prayer that she, as the bride of free Jerusalem, receive the kisses of the Bridegroom.

A good tree is known by its good fruit [cf. Matt 12.33], and ought never to be cast into oblivion, because by producing sweet fruit it has earned the sweet love of good men. A person, therefore, who does not properly embrace things that are truly delightful will, rightly, be regarded as lower than brute beasts. And so, unsullied dove of Christ, great and pure in spirit, just as good does not create evil, nor light bring forth darkness, nor sweet produce bitterness, so too you never depart from my heart. Likewise, you ought to keep me frequently in mind, since, as is well known, I am joined to you in intimate closeness of love and devotion. I do not want the flower, nursed so gently in former days, to dry up in your heart, the blossom that once vitally flourished between the two of us at the time when you were gently educating me. By that love and by the love of your beloved Spouse, I beseech and implore you to send up prayers and supplications to God both for me and for my flock and for the community that was entrusted to me by your permission. Also, I ask that you deliver us up to the prayers of all your sisters. I pray also that you work out a kind of alliance between your sisters (nay, mine also) and mine, and, when a messenger becomes available, send us a letter informing us, in Christ, what you feel about this matter, as well as any other. I myself, God willing, will not delay a visit to you when the time becomes available, so that we may speak face to face, and, hand in hand, do what is good. In this way, our ancient friendship will be strengthened. May God, Who is love [cf. I John 4.16], make it strong!

O you "who live in gardens" [Cant 8.13], give heed, and, as cordially as possible, greet for me all those who dwell with you, that is to say, my sisters, and make me joyful with your approving letter.

Hildegard's Spreading Reputation

IV

Very early on, starting, surprisingly, as early as the late forties, even before her first great book, the *Scivias*, was completed, Hildegard's fame as a woman singled out for the especial blessing of God, a seer gifted with insight into the celestial mysteries, had spread beyond the bounds of her community. Frequently this reputation was purely oral, spread by word of mouth among people who were totally ignorant of her written work, and, consequently, it sometimes was distorted into views of her as a kind of gifted clairvoyant, even fortune-teller. As a result, she began receiving petitions from all around the Christian world seeking to tap into this divine source. The largest number of letters came from people requesting information about departed loved ones; others, from people terribly disturbed by the sinful state of the world, or of their own pathetic souls; still others, from those seeking material gain through the mystical insight of this holy woman.

This letter, written as early as 1148–49, was sent to Hildegard from a young man in great distress. Mightily troubled by the state of the world, by the terrible floods of iniquity that threaten to overwhelm it, the writer feels himself so caught up in evil that he moves dangerously close to despair. In his misery, he cries out desperately to Hildegard for assistance.

Letter 20 ❧ *from Odo of Soissons*

Odo of Soissons, a broken reed, the embodiment of evil, food for the devil, sends greetings to Hildegard, saint, friend of God, bride of Christ.

It is written, "having no covering, they embrace the stones" [Job 24.8]. But in our day, alas, all the obstacles to iniquity have been removed: the stones, intended as a barrier to the road of sin; the mountains, ordained to fall upon the heads of sinners; the hills, established to bury those who have fled from Christ. The wicked deeds of men, which have run only half their course, are laid bare before God, and, if no one intervenes, they dash headlong against the stone of transgression and the rock of scandal.

As a direct result of these matters and caught up in them as I am, my lady, cut off from hope I am dashed daily against that rock, and although crushed and broken, I still dare to hope for compassion from God. And so through that same compassion of God, I entreat you not to cast me away, since I depend so fully upon you, and in the name of Him who deigned to be scorned for our sakes, do not scorn me. Please hear my plea, I beseech you, through the precious blood of Jesus Christ, your beloved Bridegroom, through that blood flowing from the cross by which He paid your dowry and made you His bride. In earnest prayer and supplication before your Bridegroom, seek to learn why, although I have cried out so often to Him from the depths and slime of my sin, He has not deigned to pull me out. Is it His will that I continue to hope for forgiveness and will He grant me a broken spirit and a contrite heart?

Commit to writing the things that you see. Farewell. Repeating my prayer again and again, I beseech you in the name of Christ not to forsake me.

Hildegard sends a note of comfort and consolation. She advises Odo to turn his mind from the inconstant and vain world, and to concentrate instead on his proper business, the salvation of his soul. Take pride also, she advises, in the work you have already accomplished for God.

Odo was appointed Cardinal-Bishop of Tuscany some twenty years later. So, perhaps, he took the consolation she offered to heart.

Letter 21 to Odo of Soissons

Because I see and hear and know all to the same effect, I write these things according to a true vision of the mysteries of God: O man, you are like a cloud that shifts back and forth and, no matter where it is, has very little light. And indeed it frequently blocks out the sun, so that its light is cut off for a long time. Thus it is written: "For behold they that go far from thee shall perish" [Ps 72.27]. The point of this verse is that those who have the day of good knowledge wither up when they turn away from it to bring forth useless things. They focus instead on the inconstancy of that darkness which, empty and barren, does not seek aid in reason. Such people are lacking in the vitality that comes from God. For Adam shone brightly in the innocence of his sanctity, but he was caught in his sin so that, turning aside from God's commandments, he perished. Then the crown of Innocence, the beautiful daughter of the King, was taken from him.

Turn your mind back again to wholesome things, and look into the fountain of dancing water [cf. John 4.14]. Keep out of matters that do not concern you, for every useless thing will wither, since it has not been planted by God. Let your mind be pure in God, keep the hunger for God's justice, stay in the straight path, and God will receive you.

Be content with the labor which you have done for God, and are still doing. But as far as you can, direct your mind and thoughts toward God. As for me, I will constantly pour out my prayers to God for you.

Hildegard frequently received letters from correspondents who confessed themselves to be horrible sinners (a conventional act of Christian humility), but this poor wretch seems to be an exceptional, excessive case of abominable sinfulness, which, however, he need not confess in detail because he knows that Hildegard, who is informed by the Spirit, knows all about them. This pitiable soul, nevertheless, wants Hildegard to inform him whether he has "any hope for salvation" or whether he is predestined for eternal death. Does Hildegard simply not deign to answer, or has her reply been lost?

Letter 22 ❦ *from a Provost*

To Hildegard, mirror of divine contemplation, G., "outcast of the people" [Ps 21.7] and provost of St. Victor in Mainz, if the sighs of a contrite, humbled heart are efficacious.

Attracted by the good aroma of your reputation and animated to the hope of salvation from the depths of sin, I request that you allow me, nurturing mother, to approach you, and lay bare my wretchedness with tears of compunction. Perhaps it is presumptuous of me—but presumptuous, I think, for the right reasons—to seek your aid and advice. I can scarcely find the words to express my misery, my confusion and shame, my tears of distress. And no wonder! For my body and spirit were sinfully polluted—worthy, it grieves me to confess, of divine chastisement by the just and merciful judgment of God, although even worse passions followed. For I have often fallen into abominable iniquity, both in thought and deed—which, however, you know well through the revelation of the Holy Spirit. Therefore, it is hardly necessary for me to write that things are not well with my soul, for the Spirit teaches you everything.

So, saintly lady, I cast myself at your feet, since "I am dust and ashes" [Gen 18.27], and with humble devotion beseech you to pray for me to the Consoler and Liberator of our souls. And please inform me whether I have any hope for salvation: am I predestined for life or foreknown for death. Please do not regard my presumption as foolishness. May the Holy Spirit, who dwells in you, grant you to respond to all these things, in answer to my prayers, according to my faith and humility. Farewell.

This letter is another one of those from a poor, disconsolate soul who seeks comfort in a word from Hildegard. The letter is eloquent testimony of Hildegard's growing fame as prophet and seer, which is spreading widely by word of mouth. "I have heard of your reputation, which is spreading abroad," Godfrey declares, and "I would walk barefoot just to hear the sound of your voice," he burbles on, though he confesses never to have read her works. And he is confident that she knows all the secrets of his heart, since she sees "all things past, present, and future."

Letter 23 ଈ *from Godfrey the Monk*

Godfrey, unworthy priest and least among the monks of St. Benedict, sends his pledge of devout obedience with all humility to the most serene and truly blessed Hildegard, endowed with the spirit of divine revelation.

"They that trust in" the Lord, "shall understand the truth: and they that are faithful in love shall rest in him: for grace and peace is to the elect" of God [Wisdom 3.9]. The truthful reports of many people have taught me and made me sure that these sacred words, uttered by divine wisdom, will be fulfilled in you. And whatever I find verified by Holy Scripture I cling to faithfully, because no word is impossible with God [cf. Luke 1.37]. Therefore, although I have never seen your divine revelations, I have heard of your reputation, which is spreading abroad, and I have never doubted its truth. And so I know in truth that because you have placed your faith in the Lord, you have understanding of His truth, and because, faithful to Him, you have rested in His love, you have received the gift of divine revelation and the spirit of heavenly consolation, and therefore achieved the peace of God's elect.

Now, therefore, because the compassion of almighty God is found more abundantly in you than in any other mortal, I do not, I want you to know, make my request to you in order to tempt you, nor to be arrogant, but to seek God's grace through you humbly. I beseech you to remember the word of the Lord: Do not despise one of my little ones [cf. Matt 18.10]. Please do not, therefore, scorn my letter on account of my insignificance, but for the love of Jesus Christ, mercifully heed my prayers, I pray. And intercede with God for my sins, and with your holy prayers lift up my life, and do not fail to chastise my negligence with a letter of admonition. For I keenly desire the rebuke of your sweetest love. Although I judge myself unworthy of a loving response from you, I desire to receive the reward of my simple trust. For I believe that all the secrets of my heart are laid bare before you by that Spirit through whom you see all things past, present, and future. Never did a day shine more brightly for me than when I came into your presence. And I would walk barefoot just to hear the sound of your voice, which would be altogether pleasant and desirable for me, if only I were worthy to hear your wondrous visions or to receive a letter from you, blessed lady.

May the almighty Father through the power of his Son, our Lord Jesus Christ, and through the accord of the Holy Spirit, deign to grant you length of days so that you may work to amend His holy Church.

Hildegard sends gentle words of consolation to Godfrey.

Letter 24 ❧ to the Monk Godfrey

The Living Light says: "O man, streams of water flow from Me to invigorate your mind. But your mind has been bound up and distressed by unstable morals in the blackness of a scudding wind. And your secret thoughts deceive you sometimes, and sometimes you are led astray by the taste of your own works. But the face of your desire turns toward Me in the joyful hope of recovery, which you are not yet able to attain by your work. Very good are those desires which build a tower on the heights of the fragrance of sweet aroma. Therefore, the angels of God rejoice because of the works produced by the creature made by the finger of God, for these works taste God by destroying the food of the unrighteousness of sinners."

Now, O knight, be strong in battle as long as you live in the body, because your enemy does not grow weary, nor does he weaken in battle. Let your works be such that the gentle Father will rejoice over you, and his Word will enlighten your spirit, and the fiery Lover will shed the ointment of salvation and the invigoration of the flower of wisdom upon you.

Although the query that occasioned this letter has not survived, it is clear that the writer has asked Hildegard about the fate of a departed soul that was dear to him. Sometimes Hildegard refuses to answer such queries, disclaiming any knowledge of such matters, but here she answers in detail.

Letter 25 ❧ to Gero, Bishop of Halberstadt

In a true vision I saw and heard these words spoken by Wisdom for the people's scrutiny: As a result of God's benevolence, as well as that just man's own merits, he is now numbered among the blessed and the just, that is, the saints.

And Wisdom says again about him: Let the winds be lifted through the four elements, and let them sound this forth with praises among the people: that he has gone before with voice raised in prayer. For when the just have completed their woeful pilgrimage and come at last to blessedness, God's grace should, justly and rightly, be praised in them, for they have been found without trace of wicked deeds committed against God's justice through infidelity or deception. That just man indeed breathed forth sighs which ascended through the mirrored eye of the cherubim to the throne of God.

In answer to a request for knowledge about future events, Hildegard responds that such things are not shown to her. Nevertheless, she answers in quite specific terms about the fate of the widow's husband, whose soul, she indicates, is in purgatory.

Letter 26 ॐ *to a Widow*

O daughter of the Creator (for this is what you are, since God Himself created you), I say to you in the love of Christ that in the vision of my soul I see many miracles of God, and, through God's grace, I understand the profundities of the Scripture, but what sorts of things lie in store for individuals are not revealed to me in that vision.

In that vision, however, I understood that your husband's soul is in great torment, although it has not been sent into perdition. This is true because although he served his own will more than he served God, he nevertheless had the will and desire in his heart to do good works, but was prevented by death from carrying out his wishes.

Dear lady, I do not presume to ask God about what lies in store for a person, because it is more profitable to the salvation of one's soul not to know such future matters, than otherwise. But I will gladly pray for you to the omnipotent God to arrange all things for the salvation of your soul and body.

Do not desist, as far as you are able, to give aid to the soul of your husband with masses, alms, and prayers every day for three years so that he may be freed from the terrible afflictions of torment through the mercy of Christ's Passion. Also, for yourself, keep faith in God, entrust everything to Him, and He will never desert you, but will preserve you in eternal blessedness.

Hildegard predicts the death of this woman's ill husband and advises her to prepare him for it.

Letter 27 ❧ to Luthgard of Karlsburg

O creature of God, Luthgard, arrange your affairs as you must, because I do not see your husband's health returning before his death. Beseech him, therefore, correct, and admonish him for the salvation of his soul, for I see great darkness in him. May God regard you so that you will live forever.

Hildegard sends an incantation to a woman to be used to alleviate her disease.

Letter 28 ❧ to Sibyl, a Married Woman of Lausanne

O Sibyl, I say these things to you in the light of true visions. You are a daughter of the woods caught up in a whirlwind of disease. But God keeps watch over you, lest your soul be lost. Therefore, trust in God. Also, place these words on your breast and on your navel in the name of the One Who disposes all things with justice: "In the blood of Adam, death was born; in the blood of Christ, death was enchained. By that blood of Christ, I command you, blood, to cease your flow."

Hildegard responds to a personal plea seeking information about the fate of the soul of a departed loved one.

Letter 29 ❧ to a Cleric

O servant of God, the soul you inquired about has not yet been freed from the pains of purgatory. Therefore, diligently pray for it to God, and rejoice, for it is reckoned by God among the number of blessed spirits. May the Holy Spirit enkindle you with His grace, and strengthen you in His service.

In answer to a priest who had apparently written her that he was being plagued by terrible nightmares, Hildegard sends out this letter of consolation, assuring him that it is by God's dispensation that he is being afflicted, in order that his "carnal thoughts will be sharply restrained." Then, in something of a contradiction, she supplies him with an exorcism to cure him of his problem.

Letter 30 ❧ to a Priest

O servant of God, you who are an ornament in Christ's office, do not fear the heaviness which rises in you on account of your terrifying dreams, for these are caused by bloody humors in conjunction with melancholia. Your sleep is troubled, but your dreams very often are not true, because the ancient deceiver (although he does not harm your physical senses) troubles you by these deceptive dreams. It is by the dispensation of God that you are chastened by such an affliction, so that through this fear all your carnal thoughts will be sharply restrained.

Every single night, place your hand on your heart, and, with sincere devotion, read the gospel "In the beginning was the Word" [John 1.1], and afterward say these words: "Lord God Almighty, Who in Your full goodness breathed the breath of life into me, I beseech You through the holy garment of the gentle humanity of Your Son (which He put on on my account) that you not suffer me to be torn apart by the bitterness of this great distress any longer, but through the love of your only begotten Son and your great mercy free me from this tribulation, and defend me from all the snares of the spirits of the air."

May the Holy Spirit make you a tabernacle of sanctification so that in the joys of supreme bliss you may live always with God.

This correspondent seeks out Hildegard with a personal plea to be healed from "a terrible affliction of body, which still torments me day and night." He was once in her presence, he reminds her, and he has every confidence that she will be able to aid him now. Hildegard's response to this plea, if one, has not come down to us.

Letter 31 ❧ from a Provisor

To Hildegard, gem of Bingen, true bride of Christ, grounded in the discipline of the Rule, H., unworthy provisor[1] of the Augustinian Rule in Hameln, with unstinting and devoted prayer for her.

In the long interval of our spiritual love, I have often wished to be in your presence, especially since I have been burdened down by a chronic illness. Once when I was in your presence, as you will remember, daughter of Christ, I was suffering a terrible affliction of body, which still torments me day and night. And just as human frailty is incapable of comprehending the vengeance of God, I do not know whether I have fallen victim to a bodily disease or a spiritual trial because of an increase in benefits. Yet "by the grace of God, I am what I am" [I Cor 15.10], because I do not cease to show almighty God the weight of my meager labor both in vigils and in prayers.

I implore you, saintly lady, to pray for an end to my suffering, if you please. Having faith in your piety, and your daughters', I beseech you to intercede with God for me. Asking your help, saintly

---

1. A provisor was a kind of administrator who attended to the secular affairs of a monastery.

lady, I pray that my disease will be rooted out through your prayers. Although "the continual prayer of a just man availeth much" [James 5.16], there is much that I cannot explain, immoderate sinner that I am, perilously overwhelmed by spiritual and physical weakness.

Please send me something in writing to inform me what the divine mysteries say I should do. Farewell, lady, and pray to your Bridegroom for me.

Hildegard seeks to answer the various questions this correspondent has transmitted to her, but she also warns him, in effect, that he should not let his imagination run away with him. His letter has not survived, but it seems that he has asked her the meaning of certain dreams he has had. Did he dream of the death of Pope Eugenius? The standard edition of the letters dates this letter as "about" 1153, the year of the pope's death. Or did the pope, after death, appear in a dream and set a fast-approaching day for the dreamer's own death—which seems to have been the purport of his question to Hildegard? Rudeger also wants to know the death-day of a fellow monk. It is no wonder that Hildegard warns him about inquiring into improper things. Rudeger had also apparently expressed certain concerns about the Eucharist, matters which Hildegard addresses at greater length.

Letter 32 🙠 to Rudeger, a Monk

A clear revelation in a true vision says: "O son of God, in the creating act by which you are a man, and through the faith expressed by your good works, acknowledge that you have no power except in God and through Him. God knows all things, and He gives full knowledge to no person, save as he foresees the need. For nobody—either in prophecy, or in the inspiration of God, or in his own wisdom—knows all things, or can say anything, save as far as God will show it to him through a miracle."

That light that I saw in your spirit in a true vision is this: that you are a son of salvation, but yet you live in great tribulation—sometimes in the weariness and weakness of the flesh, and in various thoughts, which at times lift you up to the heights and, at others, cause you to wander in secular concerns, and sometimes lead you into vainglory by means of a strange revelation, as it is written: "The Lord knoweth the thoughts of men, that they are vain" [Ps 93.11]. Beware, therefore, of inquiring rashly into your thoughts and dreams about how long you will remain on this earthly journey, for God has shown me no other signs concerning Pope Eugenius. Yet I see you terribly bound up and hence you ought to be freed in this life. God also shows me nothing about the length (or brevity) of the days of that brother that you asked me about, neither in years nor in seasons. And yet he still has time. But let him run mightily, because he is a little tepid and a little wearied in fleshly matters, and he goes astray somewhat in his thoughts. Let him show all these things to his priest in confession.

Concerning the body of Christ, I saw also that that power which descended into the womb of the Virgin (so that the Word of God became true flesh) remains up to the present day, as it is written: "Thou art my son, this day have I begotten thee" [Ps 2.7]. And that same power from the time that the Word of God became incarnate in the Virgin will remain even to the last day. I saw also that that same power appears like a red dawn in fire upon the altar. And that One Who made flesh and blood in the womb of the Virgin also makes the bread and wine on the altar flesh and blood.

Now, I also see that you, in the lifting up of your hands, are like a shifting cloud on account of your unstable thoughts, which cause you to doubt. Put such things aside and recognize who He is who works His works on the altar. And who is the one who can recount these marvels? When you think simply in this way, I see you pure like the sun, and your sacrifice is pleasing to God. And He will free your soul.

Sometimes Hildegard can be very specific and very detailed in her predictions and prophecies, as in the following letter to the abbot of Hirsau.

Letter 33 🙢 to Manegold, Abbot of Hirsau

I looked to Wisdom, and I heard and saw these words: There was a tree in Lebanon, and winter, as usual, came upon it. It is winter's nature to cause all things to wither and lose their moisture, but the root of that tree was so firmly planted in the ground that the winter was not able to destroy it. Still, the trunk of the tree was damaged somewhat by the weather. Its leaves, however, did not lose their viridity, and did not fall.

Now, father, understand that this imagery is directed to you. The monastery you ask about is like a valley set next to a field that is only slightly warm and fertile when the seed is planted, but which is yet magnificent in the part where the sun shines frequently. And the grace of God does not despise it, for it is caught up in the treadle winepress that constantly churns until the people are cleansed from their present error. And the people will become better after not too long a time.

Also, concerning that soul you asked about, it now has great merit among the saints, but, earlier, it made a serious error in judgment, which it did not recognize as such. And so in attempting to justify itself, it sought out things that were none of its business. For this reason it suffered heavy punishments. When human beings who are predestined for sanctity do not do the good works they know and understand through divine grace, God does not show the signs of his saints to them.

The death of that individual about whom you asked is not yet at hand. Moreover, your own death is also not immediately imminent. And that person you ask about had a generosity which ascended to God, and God loved him.

These are the words of Wisdom that I, poor little woman that I am, have written to you. Now I admonish you not to greatly fear the gloom which appears on the trunk of that tree I mentioned earlier, the gloom that results from the filthy, vile character of human instability. And do not withdraw from your salutary way of life, nor from your good works. Then you will live forever, and your heavenly Father will receive you in joy.

As has been seen, Hildegard received letters from all manner of people seeking personal favors from her, but none was quite so blatant or self-serving as the one seeking to engage Hildegard as a guide to hidden treasure. Here, responding to a letter that has not been preserved, Hildegard politely informs this seeker after fortune where her values lie. Nevertheless, she wishes him well. It is unfortunate that the letter has not survived; it would have been interesting to see the terms in which this odd proposal was couched.

Letter 34 to a Person Seeking Treasure

God reveals matters to me about the correction of sins and the salvation of souls, but nothing about how to find treasure, because He is more concerned with the salvation of mankind than with transitory treasure. Therefore, God has shown me nothing concerning this matter you ask me about, not even about the danger. Yet may He help you according to His will and your need.

Hildegard responds to a person—whether man or woman is unclear—who has inquired of the state of a departed loved one.

Letter 35 to a Certain Person

From that Light which I see in my soul, I saw these words: "All things are in the view of the Seeing Eye, which is God. In His view, you are a powerful whirlwind, which sometimes is sundered so that the light shines through. He sees you also as aimless in your wanderings, but that you also desire a virtuous life."

Concerning that soul that, sighing, you asked me about, I am not permitted to speak. Yet I can give some comfort, for although in its life that soul was guilty of aimlessness and sin, it nevertheless held the virtuous life in its thought, and that is faith in God. And God will never destroy the one who embraces the good things of the Lord, but will purge him by the rod of His torments.

O soul, you have the potential to love Him, if you do not look to the left. Therefore, stretch your hand out to Him, and He will aid you.

The following letter is, in a large sense, one of a kind in Hildegard's correspondence. It appears to be of an entirely spontaneous generation: no letter from the person addressed has come down to us, and nothing in Hildegard's letter suggests that it is in response to anything received. It seems most likely that Hildegard had simply heard by chance—through conventual gossip?—of this rebel nun and could not refrain from firing off this hortatory message to her. And, most strikingly, it is extremely harsh in the eternal punishment threatened to the recipient. Could it be that the situation called up disturbing echoes for Hildegard of her own past, for Hildegard, who herself was given to the Church at the tender age of eight, makes a point of referring to the person's excuse for her behavior on the basis of having been dedicated, unwillingly (as a child, perhaps?), to the Church in the first place. In any case, Hildegard, so unlike her usual merciful self, is here grim and unremitting in her condemnation for this breaking of the vows, taken willingly or not, and threatens the pangs of hell unless the person returns to her former state. It is difficult to think of this letter as anything but a purely personal outburst of emotion on Hildegard's part on learning about this lapsed nun.

Letter 36 ෴ to a Former Nun

O daughter of Adam, pay close attention, for in your adversity you are acting as Adam did, who despised his Lord and listened to that filthy worm, casting aside his honor and his angelic vestment. For this, he received hell as his inheritance, and lost Paradise. This is what you did when you cast off the celestial garment with which you had been invested, and looked back again to the pomp of this world which you had renounced. Yet you seek to excuse yourself for this action by insisting that you were, unwillingly, invested with this garment. Remember, however, that an infant is given baptism while resisting, and despite its weeping and wailing it is still made a Christian.

O dear daughter, with weeping thoughts I pray ceaselessly to God for you and for the salvation of your soul. May He deign to resuscitate you, just as He called the four-day-dead Lazarus back to life [cf. John 11.39–43]. Then, your heavenly Father will rejoice over you, saying: I have found my lost sheep, which had been carried off by the wolf [cf. Luke 15.6]. Remember that younger son who, after receiving his inheritance from his father, went into a distant country and, living there lecherously, consumed all his goods, and was reduced to such extreme poverty that he fed swine, and longed to eat the husks from their food, "and no man gave unto him" [Luke 15.11ff]. Thus, overcome as you are in this your day with fleshly desires and illicit love, you have days of peace and abundance, but it is certain that other days, and not to your liking, will come quickly to you when your enemies will surround you, and having pulled your wretched soul from your body will drag it with them to a land of pitch and sulphur, to the land of death, "covered with the mist of death," where "no order, but everlasting horror dwelleth" [Job 10.21–22], and where the "worm dieth not, and the fire is not extinguished" [Mark 9.43]. These will lay hold of your flesh which is now enslaved to your passions, and will devour it. All this will take place unless you come quickly before the face of the Lord, confessing with bitter tears of penitence, and making amends for the sins of your youth with worthy satisfaction.

Therefore, O dear daughter, I beseech you to clothe yourself again with Christ, whom you have cast aside, and flee on bended knees to God, so that He may resuscitate you from death to life before the day of your death. For your days are brief. May the benevolent Lord Jesus Christ, Who bore our sins on the cross, inspire you to true repentence, so that He may call you back to life, so that you may live forever.

As the preceding letter demonstrates, Hildegard could be a tough, even intolerant, old bird. Yet, save for those large controversies where it was imperative to be tough in order to survive, the letters are also an authentic witness to her more considerate, thoughtful, tolerant side. In the following letter, she gives advice about the proper sort of community for a nun with physical infirmities.

Letter 37 🌿 to the Nun Luitburga

O you, who are sprung from the world and born a daughter of God in Christ, know that all communities are in God's power. Therefore, because of your infirmity, seek out a smaller community for yourself, for God takes into account weaknesses, the infirmities of old age, and ways of life that are, according to human standards, restricted.

Therefore, do not impose the strict regimen of any community on yourself before you are proved in body and spirit. Offer consolation to the best of your ability to your sisters G. and M. Let them consider for themselves what is to their benefit so that they may not fail in spirit.

Now, therefore, live the religious life, and God will not abandon you.

Unlike her attitude toward the lapsed nun, Hildegard could also seek compassion for the poor, lost sinner. In this letter, she beseeches a community of monks to bring an errant brother back into the fold.

Letter 38 🌿 to a Community of Monks

Earth does not cast off earth, nor spurn that which is like unto itself. Rather, it builds it up to the best of its ability. Therefore, consistent with the aid and mercy of God, it behooves you to observe wisdom and bring back the wandering sheep to the fold [cf. Matt 18.12]. Then God will spare you in your sins, because you are all one earth.

Hildegard would fain take all vulnerable and distressed souls under her wing. Here, she exhorts a prelate to perform his duty in watching over the women in his care, since, as she says, such a duty with respect to the female sex was ordained by God. A monitory letter for those who would see Hildegard as some kind of medieval feminist.

Letter 39 ❧ to a Prelate

O servant of God, look zealously after the things God has entrusted to you so that you may bring your talent back to Him doubled in value [cf. Matt 25.16–17]. In all your exertions, flee the deceit of the ancient serpent, who seeks to deceive the person he perceives to be wise by making the act of performing good works appear foolish and burdensome.

God established that the female sex is to be governed by faithful teachers. Therefore, it is better for you to be a lit candle for them, and for yourself, and to watch over them faithfully in the fear and love of God than for you to toil in some other way. Following the example of Jesus Christ, Who laid down His life for His sheep [cf. John 10.11], continue to serve the Lord through those women (who follow your example), and do not abandon them. In this way, you will receive your reward from God through all the good works that they do by the grace of God. May the Holy Spirit so inspire you to live a useful life both for them and for yourself that you may merit to receive the reward of true bliss in eternal life.

From the Lord Himself, these words are for you: "My son, I will give you an olive branch beautifully arrayed with golden reeds by the skill of a craftsman." This branch stands for true humility, divinely ordained, for, in this, the Son of God put on a garment of flesh and went forth in a nature foreign to Himself. Therefore, humility has great strength to fight against man's deceitful, arrogant spirit; but it is maintained with the greatest difficulty. It is impossible for it not to possess an ornament of the purest gold, that is, good will, to which peace was given by the angels at the birth of the noble Son of God [cf. Luke 2.14]. This good will is, as it were, the material employed by the mighty King, with which all the virtues are adorned, and which, in accordance with its strength, extends the hand of aid in compassion to weak paupers and to all those who grieve in their miseries.

Dearest son, my God and Lord will give that branch to you, so that, through it, you may come in bliss to Him, the most high, the most humble, the most mild.

Hildegard writes to an abbess, the chief administrator of a community of nuns, and does not hesitate to intervene in the interior affairs of that community, even down to the detail of who should be fired from her office. Although she does not explicitly say so, she must have felt that the abbess was holding the reins of power all too loosely. The letter provides an interesting peek into the less spiritual side of an ill-governed community of women. Hildegard opens the letter with a personal remark about her method of communicating her visions.

Letter 40 ࿐ *to an Abbess*

O gentle lady, may the Holy Spirit so permeate you that you can maintain a humility that is resplendent in the fear and love of God, and, therefore, be able to arrange all your affairs as with a faithful friend. I say to you that never in the vision of my spirit am I wont to speak in undisguised words, but only as I am taught. Thus I always employ some kind of metaphor, as it is written, "I will open my mouth in parables: I will utter propositions from the beginning" [Ps 77.2]. God indeed has from the beginning set parables and metaphors before humankind, through which, usually, they are taught the way to salvation better than through the naked words themselves.

Regarding the priest you inquire about, God has not shown me that he is either rebellious against the justice of his situation or that he is of little worth, and so I trust that God will not withdraw His grace from him.

But let the daughters of that cloister zealously withdraw from all vanity, that snare to many, for they have renounced it for the love of God. Moreover, in your cloister there are some older women who are far too harsh, lacking the compassion they should have. On the other hand, they are too lenient on the unjust, according to their own whim. And some of the young women are vain and worship vanity, for which reason there is great strife among them, with the vain attacking the harsh, and the harsh, the vain. Yet these women are not so completely rebellious against their sacred calling that they cannot be restrained by the discipline prescribed by the Rule, even though their superior, who is neither overly harsh nor overly vain, is unable to take a stand against them, their superior who only wishes for them to live a life of sanctity. In my vision I see that it is better for the superior not to give up her position,[2] lest the troublesome sisters say, "The one we want is the one who is elected, and the one we reject is deposed." As a result, pernicious disobedience and disorder would arise in the cloister.

Beloved lady, with God's aid see to it that all these troublesome things are amended in your cloister, which, I trust in God, will come about through His compassion. That sister, the subprioress, who is causing the unrest by her own lax morals, should be removed from office, if it is your will, so as to put fear into those other sisters who are disobedient to their superiors. This should be done in accordance with the custom by which the cloister's offices are usually changed.

2. The abbess has apparently asked Hildegard about the advisability of giving up her administrative position. Although this abbess is apparently having real difficulties as an administrator, the question is not an unusual one. Hildegard received innumerable such requests. Her answer is, almost invariably, as here, stay the course.

Dear friend of God, by the love and fear you have for Him, may God make you like the glowing dawn that precedes the sun so that you may shine upon your congregation like the sun which gives light to the whole world. Strive to remove the duplicity of those who do not walk on straight paths, those who say one thing but mean another, and whose judgments are unjust. Such morals are like clouds that harm the earth, for through them the fruit of virtue withers, and such people gather friends to themselves by engaging in idle gossip. In this way, they oppose that which was established by the saints of old. They are like a dark cloud with an intemperate wind, and so it is impossible to hope that any fruit of good service can be found in them.

Sweet lady, all these matters I have referred to must be feared and prevented in every congregation as far as possible through the grace of God. Still, I trust in God that the gloom and darkness that now surround your cloister may be destroyed and crushed underfoot by the efforts already undertaken—and which will be undertaken—by your sisters within the cloister. Dearest lady, may the Holy Spirit so kindle His fire in you that, in the fear and love of God, you bring to perfection the care of those souls entrusted to you. Then you will be a bright gem in eternal bliss before God.

The following letter shows how intensely emotional the personal response to Hildegard sometimes was. This priest expresses his almost pathetic desire to see Hildegard, emoting about how he visualizes her with the eyes of his heart, and how he converses with her in his mind, even though he cannot come to her personally.

Letter 41 ❧ *from the Priest Baldemar*

To his most beloved and sorely missed lady and mother, Hildegard, Baldemar, a sinner, with his prayer that she will rejoice forever with Christ the Lord after this fragile and fallen state of life.

I will count myself blessed if I deserve to be consoled by a letter from you, saintly lady. But because it is the duty of a wise doctor to visit a wounded man frequently and to cautiously and competently cut away any superfluous or putrifying flesh lest the infection become worse later, I beg you by the love of the blessed Redeemer to inspect my wounds frequently so that, through the mercy of God and your counsel, no vestige of corruption remains in them.

O sweet and sorely missed mother, I have for a long time wished to take my staff in hand, and come to see you. O sweetest lady, I often gaze upon you with the eyes of my heart, and I speak and converse with you in my mind. I know that I have sinned against my God in His work; I know that I have sinned. Pray for me. I do not seek earthly gain, nor transitory things, but, rather, the grace of my God and the salvation of my soul. Help me! O how precious to me is the continued protection of your prayers.

In order that I may not be completely cheated of my desire, my lady, and so that I may satisfy myself, I have taken care to send this letter to you by my servant, who embraces you as lady and mother with pious love. May God give you consolation in this present life and perpetual beatitude with the saints. Amen.

It is quite astonishing to observe what authority in spiritual matters Hildegard came to represent in the eyes of her contemporaries. In the following letter, a priest asks her to inform him of the proper way to perform the Mass. The operative words here are "her" and "him," in that order. How is it that a woman is queried about this peculiarly male prerogative? Hildegard answers this letter at length, stressing the point of the Real Presence in the bread and wine, and adding that even an unworthy priest, befouled with sin, does not diminish the miracle of that service, as long as he is not prohibited from officiating at Mass by his superior. But it is only the priest's letter that concerns us here.

Letter 42 ❧ from a Priest

To Hildegard, chaste dove hiding "in the clefts of the rock" [Cant 2.14], C., a priest, least among the servants of Christ, sends the devotion of his personal prayer and whatever looks toward eternal salvation.

Because by the grace of God "your light" shines "before men" [Matt 5.16] for our salvation, I glorify your Father, Who has established you as a blazing lamp to illumine the Church, and, although I am a frail sinner, I rejoice with all my heart at your sanctity, with which you cling to the embraces of your heavenly Bridegroom by a special privilege. I want you to know, beloved lady, that night and day I long to see you face to face. I mention you constantly in my prayers, and, though you are absent in body, I embrace you frequently in my mind as though you were present. Therefore, I beseech you humbly, perfect lady, to commend me, a beggar by the wayside, to your Spouse, under Whose shadow you rest secure, lest the passing crowd restrain my cry. But drawn to the Lord by your prayers, may I merit to be illuminated and healed from the blindness of my heart [cf. Mark 10.46–52].[3]

Please also teach me about the body and the blood of Christ, wherein lies all the hope of the faithful, and reveal to me in the Lord the proper and improper ways for a priest to approach the sacrament. May the Lord Who is in all and over all [cf. Eph 4.6] reveal to you those things which comport to the glory of His holy Church. Farewell.

In this famous, personal letter, the Emperor informs Hildegard that all those things she had predicted to him while she was present in his court at Ingelheim have since come true. It is clear from the letter too that

---

[3]. Note how thoroughly the Scripture molds his thought in these last few sentences. The "beggar by the wayside," the "interference of the crowd," the "blindness," the "healing"—it is all there.

HILDEGARD'S SPREADING REPUTATION

Hildegard has been in touch with the Emperor, asking him to attend to some matter of importance to her.

Letter 43 ❧ *from Frederick Barbarossa*

Frederick, by the grace of God Emperor of the Romans and always august, sends his grace and every good to the lady Hildegard of Bingen.

We inform you, holy lady, that we now have in hand those things you predicted to us when we invited you to our presence while we were holding court in Ingelheim. We will continue to strive with all our efforts for the honor of our kingdom. Therefore, beloved lady, we sincerely beseech you, and the sisters entrusted to your care, to pour out your prayers to almighty God for us so that He may turn us to Himself as we labor on our earthly business and so that we may merit to obtain His grace.

Please be assured that with regard to that matter you directed to our attention we will be swayed by neither the friendship nor the hatred of any person, but with respect to justice alone, we intend to be equitable.

When Frederick first assumed power, Hildegard wrote him a friendly letter, congratulating him and offering advice, and, as the preceding letter indicates, they seemed, early on, to be on very good terms, and they may have always remained so. Indeed, as late as 1163 Frederick granted a charter of imperial protection "in perpetuity" to Mount St. Rupert. Yet in 1159 Frederick brought about the great schism in the Church, which lasted for eighteen years, by establishing his own anti-pope. So despite her friendly relations with the Emperor, it is not surprising to find Hildegard becoming sharply critical of him in later years. Considering Frederick's testimony to the truth of Hildegard's prophecies in the preceding letter, the denunciation and dire prediction in the following note from Hildegard must have been enough to make him sit up and take notice. The letter also demonstrates how fearless she could be, in her role as prophet, in facing up to the highest powers in the land when she felt they were going astray from God's eternal plan.

Letter 44 😊 *to Frederick Barbarossa*

He Who Is says: By My own power, I do away with the obstinacy and rebellion of those who scorn Me. Woe, O woe to the evil of those wicked ones who spurn Me. Hear this, O king, if you wish to live. Otherwise, My sword will pierce you [cf. Ex 22.24].

Oh, the audacity of this female person, telling the emperor himself, as she does in the following letter, that he is acting like a little boy.

Letter 45 😊 *to Frederick Barbarossa*

O king, it is imperative for you to have foresight in all your affairs. For in a mystic vision I see you like a little boy or some madman living before Living Eyes. Yet you still have time for ruling over worldly matters. Beware, therefore, that the almighty King does not lay you low because of the blindness of your eyes, which fail to see correctly how to hold the rod of proper governance in your hand. See to it that you do not act in such a way that you lose the grace of God.

The following letter in its terseness and allegorical obscurity gives very little information. It is included here only because it is a missive exchanged between two of the most remarkable women of their age. Hildegard writes to Eleanor of Aquitaine to comfort and encourage her in her time of "tribulations." The standard edition dates the letter anywhere from 1154 to 1170. Given Eleanor of Aquitaine's tumultuous lifetime, almost any period could have been her time of tribulation, but the letter was written before she was imprisoned by Henry II. So worse times are to come. The really burning question is whether this is a response to a letter Eleanor wrote seeking consolation and compassion from the seer. If so, it is an immeasurable loss that the letter has not come down to us.

Letter 46 😊 *to Eleanor of Aquitaine*

Your mind is like a wall battered by a storm. You look all around, and you find no rest. Stay calm, and stand firm, relying on God and your fellow creatures, and God will aid you in all your tribulations. May God give you His blessing and His help in all your works.

The following letter is important because the writer, like the Emperor earlier, informs Hildegard that everything that she had foretold to him has come to pass. Hildegard seems never to have replied, or at least her answer has not been preserved.

Letter 47 ❧ from a Provost

To Hildegard, beloved in Christ, S., unworthy provost of the brothers in Koblenz, greetings in the Lord.

Because you have always refreshed me with your consolation in all my tribulations, and because all the things that you have foretold me have come to pass, I ask you to beseech the merciful Lord to console me now in the midst of the troubles that assail me within and without. And especially, beloved and loving lady, write back to inform me whether, from the merciful Jesus, I dare have hope for the life to come.

As for the rest, be aware that I pray the Lord from the bottom of my heart that before I die I may worthily repent from my sins. Farewell.

Exorcism

V

In the year 1169, or thereabouts, Gedolphus, abbot of Brauweiler, wrote a letter to Hildegard, a woman he knew only by reputation. He wrote in despair, for he had on his hands a woman possessed of a devil, and despite all his efforts for some three long months, he had been unable to liberate her. At last, however, the devil himself had cried out that he could be cast out only by, as Gedolphus puts it, "the strength of your contemplation and the magnitude of divine revelation." Thus Gedolphus calls out desperately to Hildegard, asking her to send to him in a letter whatever revelation God may grant her concerning the matter. Although confined to her bed by sickness, Hildegard has "just enough strength," as she says, to answer his letter. Therefore, she sends out the following message immediately, containing a long and rather complicated rite of exorcism.

Letter 48 🙢 to the Abbot, Gedolphus

Hildegard to Gedolphus, abbot of Brauweiler.

Although I have been confined with a long and serious illness through the scourges of God, I have just enough strength to answer your request. What I am about to say does not come from myself, but from the One Who Is.

EXORCISM

There are various kinds of evil spirits. The demon you are inquiring about has those powers which resemble the moral vices of human beings. For this reason, he gladly dwells among people, and is not bothered by the Lord's cross, the relics of saints, or all the other things pertaining to service of God. Rather, he mocks them, and stands in no awe of them. Those things certainly he does not love, but he pretends to run away from them, just as a heedless fool discounts the threatening words directed at him by the wise. It is for such reasons that he is more difficult to cast out than other demons, for he will not be exorcised except by fasting, scourging, prayer, alms, and the very command of God himself [cf. Mark 9.28].

Hear, then, the answer, not of a human being but of the One Who Lives. Choose seven priests of good repute, recommended by the quality of their life, in the name and order of Abel, Noah, Abraham, Melchisedech, Jacob, and Aaron, for these offered sacrifice to the living God. The seventh priest will represent Christ, who offered his very self on the cross to God the Father. And with fasting, scourges, prayers, and oblations, let them celebrate Mass, and, then, clad in their priestly vestments and stoles, let them approach the suffering woman with their eyes averted. They are to stand around her, each one holding a rod in his hand in figure of that rod with which Moses struck Egypt, the Red Sea, and the rock at God's command [Ex 7.9–10.23; 14.16–29; 17.6], so that, just as, there, God revealed his miracles through the rod, so also, here, He may glorify Himself when that foul enemy has been cast out through these rods. These seven priests will represent the seven gifts of the Holy Spirit, so that the Spirit of God which in the beginning "moved over the waters" [Gen 1.2] and "breathed into his face the breath of life" [Gen 2.7] may blow away the unclean spirit from that wearied person.

And let the first one, who represents Abel, hold his rod in his hand and say, "Hear, O evil and foolish spirit, whoever you are that inhabit this person, hear these words which do not come from man but from Him Who is and Who lives, and flee, driven out at His command. Hear Him Who Is saying: I Who am without beginning but from Whom all beginnings come forth, and I Who am the Ancient of Days, I say: I through Myself am the day, Who never came forth from the sun, but from Whom the sun itself was enkindled. I am also Reason, which did not sound forth from another, but from which every rationality breathes forth. Therefore, I made mirrors for the contemplation of my face, in which I gaze upon all the miracles of my antiquity, which never fade, and I prepared those mirrors to ring forth in praise, for I have a voice like thunder, with which I move all the world in the living sound of all creatures."

And let that same priest and the other six standing around strike her lightly with their rods upon the head and upon the back, upon the breast and upon the navel and upon the reins, upon the knees, and upon the feet, and let them say: "Now, you, O satanic and evil spirit, you who oppress and torment this person, this form of a woman, depart! Through Him Who lives and Who has revealed these words through a simple person untaught in human learning, leave this person who is here present and whom you have oppressed for a long time, and in whom you still remain. For you have been commanded, and He Himself now commands you to begone. And so by this rod at the command of the True Beginning, that is, the Beginning Itself, you are commanded to harm her no further. Conjured and condemned also by the sacrifice and prayers and aid of Abel, in whose name we strike you."

And again let them strike her as above: "Conjured and condemned also by the sacrifice and prayers and aid of Noah, in whose name we strike you."

And again let them strike: "Conjured and condemned also by the sacrifice and prayers and aid of Abraham, in whose name we strike you."

And let them strike her as above: "Conjured and condemned also by the sacrifice and prayers and aid of Melchisedech, in whose name we strike you."

And again let them strike her as above: "Conjured and condemned also by the sacrifice and prayers and aid of Jacob, in whose name we strike you."

And let them strike her as above: "Conjured and condemned also by the sacrifice and prayers and aid of Aaron, in whose name we strike you."

And let them strike her as above: "Conjured and condemned also by the sacrifice and prayers and aid of the High Priest, the Son of God, to Whom all true priests have offered sacrifice and offer sacrifice still, in whose name and power we strike you."

And let them strike her again: "You, go out of this person confounded in that same confusion which was yours when you first fell from heaven like lead—and do not harm her further."

"And let the height which height never touched, and the depth which depth never plumbed, and the breadth which breadth never encompassed free her from your power and foolish iniquity and from all your arts. So, confounded, flee from her, and let her neither feel nor know you further. And just as you are cut off from heaven, may the Holy Spirit cut you off from her, and just as you are estranged from every felicity, so may you be estranged from her. And just as you never desire God, so may you never desire to return to her. Flee, therefore, flee, flee from her, devil, flee with all the evil, airy spirits, adjured through the power of eternity, which created all things and which made mankind, and through the benevolence of the Savior of humanity, which freed that same mankind, and through the fiery love that made mankind eternal. Also, condemned through the Passion, which He endured on the wood of the holy cross, and through the resurrection of life, and through that power which cast the devil from heaven into hell and freed mankind from his power, go out from this person confounded in that same confusion which was yours when you first fell from heaven like lead, and harm her no further, neither in the soul nor in any of the members of her body, as commanded by the Omnipotent, Who made and created her. Amen."

If the demon has not yet been cast out, let the second priest with all the other priests standing about follow that same order, until God helps her.

Gedolphus writes to Hildegard once again, to inform her of the outcome of the exorcism that he and his priests performed in accordance with Hildegard's instructions. The exorcism, he informs her, was—and was not—successful. But it will be best to let Gedolphus speak for himself:

Letter 49 ❧ from Gedolphus

Gedolphus, unworthy abbot, along with his brothers, to the venerable Hildegard with all due gratitude, with a prayer that she live, prosper, tread the world under foot, and whatever else more excellent that can be hoped for the handmaid of Christ.

The whole world now knows that the Lord has looked well upon you and filled you with His grace. Up until now, saintly lady, we have corresponded with you on behalf of the woman possessed by an evil spirit only through letters and messengers. Now, however, we pursue the matter through the person of that same woman, for we have sent her to you with great hope, and we devoutly add prayer to prayer that the closer she is to you in body, the more propitious you will be to her in spirit.

For conjured in accordance with the letter you sent us through the inspiration of the Holy Spirit, the demon abandoned the vessel he had possessed—but only for a brief time. Alas, he has returned, we know not through what judgment of God, and he has invaded that abandoned vessel again and now oppresses her more grievously than ever before [cf. Matt 12.43ff]. Then, when we conjured him again, mightily assailing him, at length he answered that he would not abandon his possessed vessel unless you were present in person. We are informing you of this for her sake, saintly lady, so that the Lord may accomplish what we, because of our sins, have not merited, and so that He Who rules over all may be glorified in you when the ancient enemy has been cast out. Farewell, beloved mother.

Hildegard receives the demon-possessed lady Sigewize at Mount St. Rupert—what could she do otherwise since Gedolphus peremptorily informs her in his letter that he has sent the lady along?—and there the demon is finally cast out, and dispersed. Then, in that same year of 1169, Hildegard receives a letter from a dean at The Holy Apostles in Cologne, informing her that he has heard that the demon has been cast out of his "very good friend," the lady Sigewize, for which he sends his blessings and rejoicing to Hildegard. He also inquires about the manner of procedure and the details of the rite of exorcism. He must, surely, have been disappointed with Hildegard's response, for she answers with only this brief letter, giving no specifics, and, with characteristic humility, downplaying any role that she herself played in the matter.

Letter 50 ❧ to a Dean

God created His work, but He did not establish it in one set way. Adam perished, and did not complete his full cycle, but fell asleep after noon. Then, God sent His breath into the prophets so that they might utter the truth, and thus Wisdom spoke through the mouths of those she had established, so that they might produce miracles. Next, the Apostles, through the guidance of the Holy Spirit, brought God's work to completion by faith; and their martyrdom, and the martyrdom of others, revealed the existence of God. Nowadays, the Holy Spirit has filled spiritual people, who bring the age to completion among themselves, and cultivate the angelic order.

Thus God's work is like the day. All have spoken in unison, but have clamored as individuals. At daybreak, dawn precedes the sun, and in the morning the sun's rays shine forth. At the third hour it begins to blaze with heat, and at noon it is fully ablaze. Then, about the ninth hour, its heat decreases, and toward evening the heat it had during the day comes to an end, and, finally, is hidden in the night. Thus the day is completed and rests from all its works, and if these works were completed in one set way, Mankind would be greatly displeased. Whence it is that God is called "Sabaoth," because each person is obliged to fulfill a course of this kind. In just this way God acts in all His works.

This has been the case in the woman you inquire about. On her behalf, the exalted, and the even more exalted, the lowly, and even more lowly, have spoken as one with their labors and prayers, and have clamored as individuals, in accordance with the instructions of the Holy Spirit. For some individuals have labored on her behalf through sighs of compassion; others, by prayers and vigils; and others, by fasts and scourgings. Moreover, many have given alms for her sake, and a large number of others have taken her part by helping her with all the good in their power. Others have brought this duty to completion with their great and persistent zeal. Thus, just as the day completes its cycle, all were looking to God at the same time for her sake.

Now, let us all together say: Glory to you, O Lord.

The blessing of God's grace be upon you and upon all those who have been moved to compassion for her, for, as the Lord himself says, "I will have mercy and not sacrifice" [Matt 9.13; 12.7; cf. Hos 6.6].

Appendix to Letter 50

It is all the more surprising that Hildegard is so sparse in her letter to the dean since elsewhere she speaks so openly and fully about the exorcism. In his section of the Vita, *Theodoric of Echternach supplies satisfying and rich details about the Lady Sigewize and the indelicate and scatological circumstances accompanying her liberation, citing at length from a lost autobiographical work by Hildegard. Although quite lengthy, Theodoric's narrative merits inclusion here for its substantial filling out of the teasing references in the Letters.*

"Meanwhile," Theodoric writes citing Hildegard herself, "I was informed that in the lower parts of the Rhine, at some distance from us, there was a certain noble woman possessed by the devil. I heard about her frequently. And I saw in a true vision that, by the permission of God, she had been possessed and overshadowed by a smoky black, demonic glob, which oppressed all the sensibilities of her rational spirit and did not allow her to sigh out to God in her proper senses, just as smoke or the shadow of a man or an object obscures and envelops. Hence she had lost all her normal faculties and actions, and frequently shouted out indecent things and acted in improper ways. But sometimes she was less oppressed when, by God's command, this torment diminished somewhat." . . .

"And when that woman had been brought to the holy relics of various places, the spirit that oppressed her, vanquished by the merits of the saints and the prayers of the people, cried out that he could not be cast out save by the counsel of an old woman on the upper parts of the Rhine. Having heard this, her friends brought her to us, just as the Lord willed. And this was the eighth year of her affliction."

In the preceding, Theodoric had quoted Hildegard. Then he adds the following interesting note in his own voice:

For when, after seven years, that woman was brought to Brauweiler so that she might be set free by the merits of

St. Nicholas, that evil spirit, compelled by prayers and exorcism, said that he would never leave his chosen vessel except by the counsel and help of a certain old woman on the upper parts of the Rhine (just as she herself has said above). And that evil spirit played with her name, calling her "Scrumpilgardis"[1] in derision.

Then Theodoric goes on to narrate what happened when the exorcism Hildegard had sent was read over the woman.

And when the reader came to the place at the end where it was written: "O blaspheming and scornful spirit, I, an unlearned and poor little feminine form, say to you through that Truth by which I, a poor and untaught form, saw and heard these things, and through that Wisdom I command you by the True Stability, and not by the whirlwind of your instability, to go out of this person," that wicked spirit went into a rage and screamed out such wails and horrible clamors that he struck those who were standing about with the utmost terror. And, at last, after he had raged for nearly half an hour, he abandoned the vessel he had possessed for so long, according to God's wishes.

When that woman realized that she had been liberated, she stretched out her hand to those standing near, asking to be lifted up because she had no strength. Then, she prostrated herself before the main altar of St. Nicholas, and gave thanks for her liberation. Yet while the people were observing this and raising up a loud clamor (as common people do) and giving thanks and praises to God with loud clapping, the brothers all the

1. Literally, "Wrinklegard"—old "Wrinkleface," as we might say.

while singing the hymn "Te Deum Laudamus," alas, strange to relate, that ancient enemy, by the secret judgment of God, returned and re-entered that vessel that he had left before. Then, trembling from head to foot, that woman raised herself up and, screeching and crying out, began to rave even worse than before.

Moreover, when that wicked spirit was asked how he had dared to enter God's creature again, he gave the following answer to the terrified and sorrowful people there: "I fled from the sign of the crucifix in terror, but not knowing where to go, I returned to my empty and unsealed vessel." And although he had been forced out of the woman by the aforementioned letter and the rites of exorcism, he bawled out in his rage that he would never go out again except in the presence of that old woman. Then, the clear-headed ones among them persuaded the friends and guardians of the possessed woman to bring her to the blessed virgin Hildegard. And so after receiving the blessing of the abbot and the brothers, she began to make her way there, with letters of recommendation.

Then Theodoric quotes Hildegard again:

"We were terrified upon the arrival of that woman, concerned about how we would be able to see or hear that woman about whom so many people had been troubled for so long. But God rained the dew of His sweetness upon us, and we lodged her in the sisters' quarters without any fear or trembling and without the help of any man. From then on, we did not yield to that demon in any respect whatsoever—neither for the horror nor the turmoil with which he confounded sinners, neither for the mockery nor the disgraceful words by which he sought to overcome us, and not even for his foul blast of wind. And

I saw that he had suffered three torments on account of that woman: first, when she was brought to the various places of the saints; second, when the common people gave alms for her; and, third, when, by the grace of God, he was compelled to leave because of the prayers of the spiritual people. And so from the Purification of St. Mary until Easter Sunday, we, along with the people of both sexes living in our region, labored on her behalf with fasts, prayers, alms, and scourging of the body.

"Meanwhile, compelled by the power of God, the unclean spirit, against his will, uttered many things about salvation through baptism, the sacrament of the body of Christ, the danger incurred by the excommunicated, and the damnation of the Cathars and those like them—all to his own confounding but to the glory of Christ in the presence of the people, so that many became stronger in the faith, and many more ready to atone for their sins. But when I saw in a true vision that he was about to declare false things, I immediately silenced him, at which, silently, he gnashed his teeth at me. Yet when he spoke the truth I did not, for the sake of the people, prohibit him from speaking.

"Finally, that holy Sabbath came, when the baptismal font was being consecrated by the breath of the priest which he breathed upon the font, and by the words which the Holy Spirit imparted to the rationality of mankind and to the doctors of the Church, since in the beginning of creation the Spirit of the Lord moved the waters, as it is written, "the spirit of the Lord moved over the waters" [Gen 1.2]. At that time that woman was there, and seized with great fear, she shook so hard that she made a hole in the ground with her feet, and frequently gave out a blast of breath from that horrible spirit that oppressed her.

Soon, in a true vision I saw and heard that the might of the Most High, which overshadowed (and always overshadows) holy baptism, said to the demonic creature afflicting that woman, "Go, Satan, go out of the tabernacle of this woman's body, and give place in it to the Holy Spirit!" Then, the unclean spirit came out through the private parts of the woman with a horrible sound of evacuation. Thus she was liberated and remained healthy in body and soul for as long as she lived in this world. And when this was afterward made known to the people, they all said 'Glory to you, Lord' in songs of praise and words of prayer."

Family

VI

The following letter is from Hildegard's nephew, who writes to inform her of his election as archbishop of Trier. The interest in the letter lies elsewhere, however. In his triumph, Arnold cannot, apparently, resist making invidious remarks about his brother, Hildegard's other nephew, Wezelinus, who is only prior of St. Andrew's. The two brothers are clearly—or this brother, certainly—in contention for the affection of their famous aunt. So it goes with saints of large families! The other point of interest in the letter is the fact that Arnold has become aware of Hildegard's exorcism of the demon from Sigewize and requests information about the procedure.

Letter 51 ❦ *from Arnold, Archbishop of Trier*

Arnold, by the grace of God humble archbishop-elect of Trier, sends greetings and love to his beloved kinswoman in Christ, Hildegard of St. Rupert, from Him who is salvation and love.

 Friendship among relatives is a heavenly thing, because old age neither thwarts nor weakens it, and when it is true, it does not stagnate, but, rather, grows and improves daily. And so since we have embraced in the arms of true love from our earliest years, I am surprised that you have more regard for a flatterer than for a true friend, since the prophet says, "But let not the oil of the sinner fatten my head" [Ps 140.5]. We consider our brother, the prior of St. Andrew's, as your flatterer, but we wish to be considered your true friend.

But because we know our success is a source of joy for you, we thought that you, beloved, should be notified that through God's grace our situation has improved. Still, because that which one regards as a punishment is no blessing, we declare before God and you that the position to which we have been called (against our will, God knows) was never, as is usual in such cases, a source of temptation or comfort to us, because our ignorance, our fragility, laments our insufficiency and deplores our infirmity. And because we do not know who has called us to such an office, we are afflicted by great anxiety. If we knew it to be God, we would have faith that He who had begun a good work in us would also bring it to perfection [cf. Phil 1.6], since our promotion to this office resulted from necessity rather than any virtue of our own.

And we know that "God in his holy place" [Ps 67.6] has worked salvation among you by visiting his people [cf. Luke 7.16] to mercifully liberate a woman possessed by the devil. Thus we earnestly beseech you to give an account of the method by which that liberation was achieved. Moreover, whenever you look to the True Light, please impart to us some saving grace through your letters, and, after the example of Moses, intercede for us by lifting up your hands to the rock of refuge, while we fight against Amalech in the valley of worldly miseries [cf. Ex 17.10].

We are writing back to you in the presence of the abbot of St. Eucharius, our faithful and beloved friend, and he has helped us by seasoning our words with his sweetness. Therefore, we also ask that you send your response back through him.

Hildegard responds to Arnold at length, but not, perhaps, as he had expected. She begins her letter with a pointed exhortation against "the falling sickness of pride," the sin of "the first angel, Satan," for she, clearly, has seen the vaunting pride of place peeping through Arnold's façade of humility. She continues her "sermon" for four succeeding paragraphs, the subtheme of which is pride. At last, in the final paragraph she addresses, briefly, the matter of the exorcism.

Letter 52 to Arnold, Archbishop of Trier

O, you are a tree planted by God, just as Paul says: All power is from God [cf. Rom 13.1], because, according to the highest authority, every power has been named in the invocation of His name, and through that invocation a tree derives its viridity from the honor of His name. May you preserve yourself from that which is not of God and which is done with the left hand, lest you fall in the falling sickness of pride, like the first angel, Satan, who set himself in opposition to God to steal furtively that honor which many people today willfully snatch for themselves, totally disregarding the means to that end. Such an attitude is nothing in God's eyes, because "without him was made nothing" [John 1.3], and thus God destroys whatever stands apart from Him.

Therefore, as far as you are able though God's grace be solicitous to give testimony to the people through God's commandments, which are as luxuriant as the leaves of a tree. For the burden of your office has many tribulations, such as poverty, which binds you in, because riches and money do not love heavenly things. In this way, God reins in man's desires so that he will sigh for heaven, his homeland. Thus it is fitting that a poor man love a poor man and a rich man acknowledge a rich man, because wisdom gives a ring to the poor man, but denies an earring to the rich.

Wherefore, with regard to your office, keep this in mind: "I have not hid thy justice within my heart: I have declared thy truth and thy salvation" [Ps 39.11]. Here is the interpretation of this passage: God's Justice does not conceal herself, but makes her paths wide and is not ashamed to run on them. Justice also does not hide her wounds by preferring evil to good, but Injustice says that life is hell, and that one must run in both directions at once. Justice, on the other hand, does not steep herself in this fallacy, nor does she kiss Injustice with a multiplicity of words; rather she tramples it underfoot. Likewise, Truth does not praise those works which are done apart from God, but, like a brave knight, prepares herself to oppose them in battle.

Now let Justice be your shield, and dress yourself in her truth, as with a breastplate, so that you may appear well armed before God and not a fugitive in the company of vanity, and learn to suck the breasts of Justice. Also, learn to heal the wounds of penitent sinners with mercy, just as the great Physician has bequeathed to you a salutary example for restoring the people to health.

For through the instruction of His name, you have been placed in the viridity of that blessed man who did not listen to the wicked devil, wicked indeed because he did not love good. Beware of boasting in your treasure, for in the end money is deceitful, because it fails one as easily after one year as after thirty. But rejoice on Mount Zion, where the help of the Most High is eternal in eternity, and where every spirit praises the Lord.

Be, also, an ivory mountain, from the windows of which spears fly in the upright judgment of justice against your adversaries. Run also to the heights of the law and justice of God, like a mountain goat, lest you fall unarmed through instability, and may your sons rise up from the side of the Church and cry out to you for the food of justice. And so learn good doctrine so that you may satisfy them.

As you asked, I have looked to the True Light, and I could scarcely see the beginning of good works. And so, now, be more zealous in doing good works so that, afterward, I may write more things to you by the grace of God. And be a faithful friend to your soul, so that you may live forever.

Finally, concerning the possessed woman you inquired about, we have seen many miracles which are impossible to put into writing now. But we know that the breath of the devil grew weaker and weaker day after day until he came forth at last and the woman was freed from the weakness caused by the devil. And during the time she was possessed, she suffered from an infirmity that, at that time, she was unaware of. But now she has recovered fully in both body and soul.

Hildegard came from a very large family, and she herself being the tenth child, she was offered as a tithe to the Lord, at least if we are to believe Guibert of Gembloux. Here, she writes to one of her brothers exhorting him to quit being nasty to another. It is interesting to see that even saints have messy family matters with which they have to deal.

Letter 53 to Her Brother Hugo

The Church frequently recounts miracles, but sometimes they move beyond truth into derision. Therefore, I admonish you not to accuse your brother Roricus unjustly in your heart and not to move beyond the bounds in speaking evil words about him. God knows that you are not acting correctly in this matter.

Therefore, beware lest the Lord find you guilty in this wrath of yours and other similar matters. May God have mercy on you in all your sins.

A Fellow Visionary

VII

Sometime after 1152, Hildegard received the following letter from her younger contemporary and fellow visionary, Elisabeth of Schönau. Having learned of Hildegard's fame as a holy woman who had the mysteries of heaven opened up to her by divine visions, Elisabeth sought her out for support and advice. Aside from just a general need to share with the older, more experienced woman, the main purpose of the letter is to enlist Hildegard's assistance in quelling the false rumors that have, as she says, been spread about her. As a result of this letter and at least one other that has been preserved, as well as a personal visit with the saint, Elisabeth became a kind of protégée of Hildegard's, the older woman taking the younger under her wing and offering comfort and support. Yet Elisabeth's visionary experiences were totally different from Hildegard's, the kind, in fact, that Hildegard always sought to distance herself from. Elisabeth was a true mystic. She received her visions in a kind of fit of ecstasy, losing all consciousness of the world around her and participating actively with the figures in her visions, as in her description of having been visited by the angel of the Lord, who severely scourged her "so that for three days thereafter I suffered from that beating in my whole body." In sharp contrast, Hildegard is always distanced from her visions, which she sees as a series of pictures projected, as it were, on a distant screen as wide as the universe, and she always stresses that she sees these things fully conscious "with eyes wide open." The letter is somewhat discursive and rambling, but it is interesting to hear from one of Hildegard's contemporaries who, at least as she felt, shared her temperament.

Letter 54 ⁂ *from Elisabeth of Schönau*

To the lady Hildegard, venerable mistress of the brides of Christ in Bingen, Elisabeth, a humble nun, sends her devoted prayers with all esteem. May the grace and consolation of the Most High fill you with joy because you have been kindly sympathetic to my distress, as I have understood from the words of my confessor, whom you have diligently advised with regard to my consolation. For just as was revealed to you about me, as you said, I have been disturbed, I confess, by a cloud of trouble lately because of the unseemly talk of the people, who are saying many things about me that are simply not true. Still, I could easily endure the talk of the common people, if it were not for the fact that those who are clothed in the garment of religion cause my spirit even greater sorrow. For stirred by I don't know what spirit, they ridicule the grace of the Lord in me, and they have no fear of making hasty judgments about things that they have no understanding of. I hear too that letters are circulating under my name about the Spirit of God. They have slandered me by claiming that I have prophesied about the day of judgment—which, certainly, I have never presumed to do, since such knowledge is beyond the ken of any human being. But let me inform you of the cause of this talk, so that you may judge for yourself whether I have said or done anything presumptuously in this matter. As you have heard from others, the Lord has poured out His mercy upon me beyond what I deserve or could even hope to deserve. So much is this true that He has frequently deigned to reveal to me certain heavenly mysteries. Through His angel, He has frequently disclosed to me what sort of things are about to befall His people in these days unless they do penitence for their sins, and He has commanded me to announce this openly. Seeking to avoid arrogance and not wishing to spread novelties, I sought, to the best of my ability, to keep all this hidden. Yet on a Sunday when I was, as usual, in a state of ecstasy [cf. Acts 11.5], the angel of the Lord stood before me and said, "Why are you hiding gold in the mud? This is the word of God which has been sent to the world to be spoken by you, because they have turned their faces away. For the word of God should not be hidden but made manifest to the praise and glory of our Lord and to the salvation of His people." And after he had said this, he lifted a scourge up over me, and as if in great wrath he struck me harshly five times, so that for three days thereafter I suffered from that beating in my whole body. Then, he placed his finger on my mouth, and said, "You will be silent until the ninth hour, but then you will make known everything the Lord has worked in you." Therefore, I remained quiet until the ninth hour. Then, I made a sign to my superior to bring me a certain little book that I had hidden in my bed, a book which contained a partial account of the things the Lord had worked in me. When I put this book into the hands of my lord abbot, who had come to visit me, my tongue was loosed, and I said, "Not to us, O Lord, not to us; but to thy name give glory" [Ps 113b.1]. After this, I also revealed to him other matters which I had not wished to commit to writing, about, for example, the mighty vengeance of the Lord which, as I learned from the angel, was soon to come upon the whole world. I entreated him earnestly, however, to keep what I had told him to himself. Yet he commanded me to take the matter up in prayer and ask the Lord to disclose to me whether He wanted me to keep silent about those things or not. Then, after I had devoted myself to urgent prayer concerning this matter for a long time, during the season of Advent on the feast of St. Barbara in the first vigil of the night, I fell into an ecstasy, and the angel of the Lord stood before me, and said: "Cry out mightily, and say 'alas' to all people because the whole world has become dark. And say to them: Rise up, for He who formed you from the dust has called you, and He says, Repent, for the kingdom of God is at hand" [cf. Matt 3.2; 4.17]. Persuaded by these words, my abbot undertook to reveal this message to the masters of the church and men of religious calling. Some of them received it reverently. Others, however, did not, but spoke slanderously about my angel, saying that he was a deceptive spirit disguised as an angel of light [cf. II Cor 11.14]. Therefore, they laid an oath of obedience upon me, and commanded me, upon his next appearance, to adjure him in the name of the Lord to tell me whether he was a true angel of God or not. Believing this to be presumptuous, I received this command with great fear. Then, on a certain day, when I was in an ecstasy, he appeared before me in his customary fashion. And, trembling, I said to him: "I adjure you in the name of God the Father, the Son, and the Holy Spirit, to tell me truthfully whether you are a true angel of God and whether those visions I saw in my state of ecstasy and heard from your mouth are genuine." He answered in reply, "Be assured that I am a true angel of God, and that the visions you have seen in your ecstasy and heard from my mouth are genuine, and they will surely come to pass unless God is reconciled to man. And I am the one who has labored with you this long time." After this, on the vigil of the Epiphany, my lord[1] appeared to me again while I was at prayer, but he stood at a distance and kept his face turned away from me. Perceiving his indignation, therefore, I said fearfully to him, "My lord, if I annoyed you when I adjured you, do not, I beg you, impute the fault to me. Please turn to me again, and do not be angry with me, because I was constrained by the necessity of obedience, and I did not dare to disobey the command of my superior." After I had wept profusely with words of this sort, he turned to me and said, "You have shown contempt for me and my brothers because you distrusted me. Therefore, know for certain that you will never see my face again, nor hear my voice, unless we and the Lord have been appeased." And I said, "My lord! How

---

1. That is, the angel.

can you be appeased?" He said, "Tell your abbot that he is to celebrate the divine office devoutly in honor of me and my brothers." Thus after the rites of the mass had been celebrated not just once but several times by both the abbot and the other brothers in honor of the holy angels, and the sisters had, at the same time, honored them with reading the Psalms, my lord appeared to me again, placated, and he said to me, "I know that what you did was done in love and obedience, and, therefore, you have attained pardon, and I will visit you even more frequently than before." After this, when my abbot was making arrangements to go to a certain place to ask permission of the clerics dwelling there to preach to the people the Lord's warning to repent so that the wrath of God would be turned from them, he came first to pray the Lord, along with all of us, to deign to reveal to His handmaiden whether the words which had now begun to become manifest should be more widely divulged or not. Then, while he was celebrating the divine mysteries, and we were all praying devoutly, suddenly my joints went slack, and I became dizzy and fell into a state of ecstasy. And, behold, the angel of the Lord stood before me, and I said to him, "My lord, remember what you said to me, your handmaiden, that the word of God had been sent into the world through my mouth, not to be hidden but to be revealed to the glory of God and the salvation of His people. Reveal to me now what must be done about that word of warning which you disclosed to me. Is it now sufficiently well known or must it be preached further?" But he looked at me sternly, and said, " 'Do not tempt God' [cf. Matt 4.7; Luke 4.12], for those who tempt Him will perish. You are to say to the abbot: 'Do not be afraid, but finish what you have started. They are truly blessed who hear the words of your exhortation and observe them, and they will not be offended at you.' But impart this to him also, that he is not to alter the method of preaching he has used so far. I have been his advisor on this point. Say to him to give no heed whatsoever to those who, out of ill will, speak doubtfully about the things which have been done through you. Rather, let him bear in mind what has been written, that nothing is impossible with God" [cf. Matt 19.26]. Animated by these words, therefore, the abbot went to the place he had arranged to go, and exhorted those who had awaited his arrival to repent. He announced that the wrath of God would come upon all unless they zealously forestalled it by the fruits of penitence [cf. Matt 3.8]. Despite the controversy in this matter, he detailed in his sermon the kind of plagues that threatened the world. And it so happened that many who had scorned this message before fearfully gave themselves over to penitence throughout the whole Lenten season, and became zealous in their alms and prayers. At that time a certain person, induced by some kind of zeal, sent a letter to Cologne in the name of my abbot—though he himself was ignorant of it, God knows—a letter in which terrible threats were recounted in the hearing of all the people. Therefore, although some foolish persons mocked us, the prudent, as we hear, reverently heeded the message, and did not fail to venerate God with the fruits of penitence. It happened that on the fourth day before Easter I had endured great bodily suffering and then entered a state of ecstasy. Then the angel of the Lord appeared to me, and I said to him, "Lord, what will be the outcome of this message that you spoke to me?" And he answered, "Do not be grieved or disturbed if the things I predicted to you do not occur on the day which I had set, because the Lord has been appeased by the repentance of many." After this, on the sixth day at about the third hour, I went with great pain into a state of ecstasy, and again the angel stood before me, and said, "The Lord has seen the affliction of His people and has turned from them the wrath of His indignation." I said to him, "What then, my lord? Will I not be an object of derision to all the people to whom this word was revealed?" And he replied, "Whatever happens to you on this occasion, endure it all with patience and kindness. Diligently heed Him Who, although He created the whole world, endured the derision of men. Now, the Lord is putting your patience to the test."

A FELLOW VISIONARY

My lady, I have explained the whole sequence of events to you so that you may know my innocence—and my abbot's—and thus may make it clear to others. I beseech you to make me a participant in your prayers, and to write back to me some words of consolation as the Spirit of the Lord guides you.

In the following letter, Hildegard offers consolation—and affirmation, for she assures Elisabeth that those inspired by God can expect afflictions from the devil. On the other hand, there is surely some bit of warning, mild though it is, in Hildegard's exhortation to Elisabeth to be like a trumpet, which sounds not of its own, but only by the breath of another, an image which Hildegard then, happily, applies to herself.

Letter 55 ❧ to Elisabeth of Schönau

I, a poor little form of a woman and a fragile vessel, say these things not from myself, but from the Serene Light: Man is a vessel which God has fashioned for Himself, and which He has imbued with His inspiration so that He might complete all His works in him. For God does not work as man does, but all things are brought to perfection by His command. Vegetation, forests, and trees appeared, and the sun, moon, and stars came forth, in order to serve mankind. The waters brought forth fish and birds. Herds and beasts also arose, all to serve man, as God commanded.

Of all creation, however, man alone did not acknowledge Him.[2] For although God gave him great knowledge, man elevated himself in his own spirit, and turned away from God. God had looked on

---

2. This idea is not, of course, new with Hildegard. It was perhaps given the most notable—certainly, the most influential—expression in twelfth-century thought by Alanus de Insulis in *The Complaint of Nature*. Alanus's vision of a monumental personified Nature, on whose robe was figured all the creatures of the world, with a rip in the garment only in that place where man was represented, is the most famous literary, allegorical representation of this idea.

103

man to perfect all His works in him, but the ancient deceiver deluded him, and through the delight of an unseasonable wind tainted him with the sin of disobedience when he sought out more than he should have.

Ach! Woe! Then all the elements became entangled in the alternation between light and darkness, just as man himself did in transgressing against God's commands. But God "irrigated" certain men so that man would not be totally mocked. For Abel was good, but Cain was a murderer [cf. Gen 4.2ff]. And many saw God's mysteries in the light, but others committed multitudinous sins until the time arrived when God's Word shone forth, as it is said: "Thou art beautiful above the sons of men" [Ps 44.3]. Then the "Sun of justice" [Mal 4.2] came forth and illumined men with good works both in faith and deed, just as the dawn comes first, and the other hours of the day follow until the night comes. So, O my daughter Elisabeth, the world is in flux. Now the world is wearied in all the verdancy of the virtues, that is, in the dawn, in the first, the third, and the sixth—the mightiest—hour of the day. But in these times it is necessary for God to "irrigate" certain individuals, lest His instruments become slothful.

Listen now, O my anxious daughter. The arrogant deception of the ancient serpent sometimes wearies those persons inspired by God. For whenever that serpent sees a fine jewel he hisses and says, What is this? And he wearies that jewel with the many afflictions which distress a blazing mind longing to soar above the clouds, as if they were gods, just as he himself once did.

Listen again: Those who long to complete God's works must always bear in mind that they are fragile vessels, for they are only human. They must always bear in mind what they are and what they will be. They must leave to Him who is of heaven the things of heaven, because they are exiles ignorant of the things of heaven. They can only sing the mysteries of God like a trumpet, which only returns a sound but does not function unassisted, for it is Another who breathes into it that it might give forth a sound. But let them put on the breastplate of faith [cf. I Thess 5.8], those who are mild, gentle, poor, and afflicted, like the Lamb, for they are the sound of His trumpet, and in character they are like guileless children. For God always scourges those who sound His trumpet, but according to His own good purpose, He foresees that their fragile vessel will not perish.

O my daughter, may God make you a mirror of life. I too cower in the puniness of my mind, and am greatly wearied by anxiety and fear. Yet from time to time I resound a little, like the dim sound of a trumpet from the Living Light. May God help me, therefore, to remain in His service.

A Sermon

VIII

On her third preaching tour, which took place sometime between 1161 and 1163 (when she was in her mid-sixties, be it noted), Hildegard preached a fiery sermon to the clerics in the cathedral city of Cologne. The following letter from the dean and clerics of the cathedral is a personal plea for Hildegard to put down in writing the words that they had received only orally at that time, for they hold her words, as they say, to be "from the very oracle of God." What greater acclaim could Hildegard have achieved: a woman preaching to a male audience, castigating them, in no uncertain terms, for their sins—and making them like it!

Letter 56 ❧ *from the Clerics of Cologne*

Philip, unworthy dean, and the entire chapter of the cathedral of Cologne send greetings to that venerable partaker of the portion which Mary chose [cf. Luke 10.42], Hildegard of St. Rupert in Bingen, who, in the purity of her heart, gazes upon God in the present life, and, in the life to come, face to face [cf. I Cor 13.12].

Because we esteem your maternal piety, we want to inform you that after your recent visit to us at God's command when, through

A SERMON

divine inspiration, you revealed the words of life to us, we were greatly astonished that God works through such a fragile vessel, such a fragile sex, to display the great marvels of His secrets.

But "the spirit breatheth where he will" [John 3.8]. For since it is abundantly clear that the Spirit has chosen a dwelling pleasing to Himself in your heart, understandably we come to you in admiration as if to the living temple of God to offer up prayers, and we seek responses of truth from your heart, as if from the very oracle of God. We sincerely beseech you, blessed lady, to commend our desires earnestly to God, since they pertain to the welfare of souls. And if your soul, clinging to God as usual, sees anything concerning us in a true vision, please inform us in a letter. We further request that you commit to writing and send us those things that you said to us earlier in person, since, given over as we are to carnal lusts, we all too readily ignore spiritual matters, neither seeing nor hearing them.

Farewell, beloved lady. May God whom you love with your whole heart be with you.

This letter is Hildegard's response to the Cologne clerics. Since it is a sermon, it scarcely qualifies as a personal letter, and yet what a personal sermon it is, directed pointedly at that male audience directly in front of her: You have sinned, before God, to your shame; you have been woefully negligent in your divinely assigned duty; you have offended God by your iniquities! The sermon is consummately Hildegardian in its stress on the larger universe as a mirror of the little world of man. It is a delight to read. No wonder the clerics wanted their own copy.

Letter 57 to the Clerics of Cologne

"The one who was, and is, and is about to come" [Apoc 1.4] speaks to the shepherds of the Church: He Who Was was about to make all creation, so that it had the testimony of testimonies in itself by doing all His works just as He wished. He Who Is made all creation and showed the testimony of testimonies in all His works, so that each

107

created thing appeared. He Who Is About To Come will purge all things, and He will re-create them in a different way, and He will wash away all the blemishes of the times and the seasons, and He will make all things ever new, and after the purgation He will reveal unknown things. From Him the wind blows, saying: lacking no power, I have set the firmament with all its ornaments, with eyes to see, ears to hear, a nose to smell, a mouth to taste. For the sun is like the light of His eyes, the wind like the hearing of His ears, the air like His fragrance, the dew like His taste, exuding viridity like His mouth. The moon marks the times of the seasons, and reveals knowledge to men. And the stars, which seem to be rational, are indeed so, because they are circular, just as rationality embraces many things. I shored up the four corners of the earth with fire, cloud, and water, and in this way I joined together all the boundaries of the world like veins. I formed rocks from fire and water like bones, and I established earth from moisture and viridity like marrow. I stretched out the abyss like feet which hold up the body, around which the exuding waters serve as its foundation. Everything was made in this way so as not to fail. If the clouds did not have fire and water, there would be no firm bond, and if earth did not have moisture and viridity, it would crumble like ashes. And if the other luminaries did not have the light of the sun's fire, they would not shine through the waters, but would be invisible.

These are the materials for the instruction of mankind, which he comprehends by touching, kissing, and embracing, since they serve him: by touching, because a man remains in them; by kissing, because he gains knowledge through them; by embracing, because he exercises his noble power through them. Thus mankind would have no freedom of possibility if they did not exist with him. So, they with mankind, and mankind with them.[1]

---

1. This letter is perhaps Hildegard's fullest, most detailed expression of man the microcosm. In the remainder of the letter, note the intricate ways she uses to re-express the idea of the larger world of the universe reflected in the little world of man.

A SERMON

O my children, you who feed my flocks as the Lord commanded, why do you not blush, since none of the creatures desert the precepts they received from the Master but, rather, bring them to perfection? I set you like the sun and the other luminaries so that you might bring light to people through the fire of doctrine, shining in good reputation and setting hearts ablaze with zeal.

I did this in the first age of the world. For I chose Abel, I loved Noah, I instilled in Moses the precepts of the law, I established as prophets those who most loved me. Thus Abel prefigured the priesthood; Noah, the papal office; Moses, the regal messenger; and the prophets, the many other offices. Moreover, Abel poured forth his brightness like the moon, because he revealed the time of obedience in his burnt offering; and Noah, like the sun, because he brought the edifice of obedience to perfection; and Moses, like strong planets, because he received the law through obedience. And the prophets, like the four corners which hold up the boundaries of the world, persevered mightily when they rebuked the whole world for its terrible iniquity, and thus made God known.

But your tongues are silent, failing to join in with the mighty voice of the resounding trumpet of the Lord, for you do not love holy reason, which, like the stars, holds the circuit of its orbit. The trumpet of the Lord is the justice of God, which you should meditate upon zealously in holiness, and through the law and obedience of your office make it known to the people at the proper time with holy discretion, rather than pounding them mercilessly with it.

But you are not doing this on account of the waywardness of your own will. Thus the luminaries are missing from the firmament of God's justice in your utterances, as when the stars do not shine, for you are the night exhaling darkness, and you are like people who do not work, nor even walk in the light because of your indolence. But just as a snake hides in a cave after it has shed its skin, you walk in filth like disgusting beasts.

Oh woe, just as it is written: you ought to be "Mount Sion in which thou hast dwelt" [Ps 73.2]. For, blessed and sealed in the celestial persons, you ought to be the little habitation redolent of myrrh and incense, in which God also dwells. But you are not so. Rather, you are quick in your pursuit of adolescent lust, incapable, like children, of even speaking of your own salvation. You do whatever your flesh demands. Wherefore it is said about you: "Lift up thy hands against their pride unto the end; see what things the enemy hath done wickedly in the sanctuary!" [Ps 73.3]. For the power of God will crush and destroy your necks which have become stiff with iniquity, for they have been puffed up as with the breath of the wind, since you neither know God nor fear men. Indeed, rather than despising iniquity, you have no desire to cast it out of yourselves. You do not see God nor even wish to do so, but you look at your own works and judge them according to your own standards, that is to say, by doing or abandoning at your own pleasure.

Oh, what great evil and enmity this is! that a person is unwilling to live an upright life, either for God's sake or mankind's, but, rather, seeks honor without work and eternal rewards without abstinence. Such a one, in his supposed sanctity, vainly longs to cry out, as the devil does, I am good and holy. But this is not true.

What do you say now? You do not have eyes,[2] since your works do not shine before men with the fire of the Holy Spirit, and you do not meditate on good examples for them. Therefore, the firmament of God's justice in you is lacking in the light of the sun, and the air has lost the edifice of virtues, sweetened by a pleasing fragrance. Whence it is said: "They have eyes and will not see. They have noses and will not smell" [Ps 115.5–6]. For just as the winds blow and penetrate the whole world, so should you be mighty

---

2. Note how nicely she carries out her microcosm/macrocosm thought pattern ("For the sun is like the light of His eyes" just above) and how well she ties it into the biblical passage cited just below.

winds teaching all people, just as it is said: "Their sound has gone forth into all the earth" [Ps 18.5]. You are worn out by seeking after your own transitory reputation in the world, so that, at one moment, you are knights, the next slaves, the next mere, jesting minstrels, so that in the perfunctory performance of your duties you sometimes manage to brush off the flies in the summer.

Through the teaching of the Scriptures, which were composed through the fire of the Holy Spirit, you ought to be the corners of the Church's strength, holding her up like the corners that sustain the boundaries of the earth. But you are laid low and do not hold up the Church, retreating instead to the cave of your own desire. And because of the tedium brought on by your riches, avarice, and other vain pursuits, you do not properly teach your subordinates, nor indeed do you even allow them to seek instruction from you. For you say, We can't do everything. But you ought to steep them in the precepts of the law, and thereby restrain them, lest any of them, in his frailty (his marrow, as it were), do whatever he wishes, just as the earth is steeped and restrained by humidity and viridity, lest it turn to ashes. On account of you, however, they are scattered like ashes and always do whatever they wish.

You ought to be a pillar of fire going before them [cf. Ex 13.21] and crying out to them, performing good works before them, saying: "Embrace discipline, lest at any time the Lord be angry, and you perish from the just way" [Ps 2.12]. For the Lord's law consists of discipline through love and fear. Thus both natures—the spiritual and the carnal—must be exercised righteously, lest the Creator threaten those He has created, because they are not walking in His ways.

But you are deceiving yourselves when you say, We have no control over any of them, because if you were to chastise your subordinates properly through the reason which God gave you, they would not dare to resist the truth, but, as far as they could, they would say that your words are true. But because you are not doing this, it is said of you: "They were troubled, and reeled like a drunken man; and all their wisdom was swallowed up" [Ps 106.27]. For you are troubled, since you have no regard for the good in yourselves, and thus do not walk properly. You reel and stumble, since your works do not give you the right answer, and, like a drunk man, you do not know what you are doing. This is because you willfully do whatever you want. Whence all the wisdom which you sought so hard to find in Scripture and in instruction has been swallowed up in the pit of your own will, since you did those things you learned by touching and tasting merely to fulfill your own desires in the fatness of your flesh, just like a child who does not know what he is doing because he is a child. Therefore it is again said to you: Unlike the feet that hold up the body, you are not presenting a wholesome and stable example of morality before the people, so that you can surround them by the Scriptures, just as the abyss is completely surrounded by oozing waters. But you say, We don't have time now for talking, and there is not even time for us to be heard as there used to be. And I reply, Abel did not fail to perform his sacrifice, despite his brother's hatred, but he presented it to his Lord, even though he was killed for it. And Noah sweated profusely, greatly dismayed at the terrible judgment that all creation was to be drowned, for he greatly feared death when he stood above the cloud. When others saw him, they cried out, What is that fool doing? The winds will surely destroy him. Nevertheless, he fulfilled God's command. Similarly, Moses the lawgiver suffered cruelly at the hands of his brothers and neighbors, but, for all that, he did not abandon the law. Rather, he fulfilled God's commands. Also, in their obedience to God, the prophets were killed by infidels, as if by rabid wolves. But you are unwilling, in this short and comfortable life, to endure injuries at the hands of the people, and thereby you are laying up infinite torments for yourselves. You ought to be the day, but you are the night. For you will be either the day or the night. Choose, therefore, where you wish to take your stand. You are not the sun and moon and stars in the firmament of God's law and justice. Rather, you are the darkness, in which you lie as if you are already dead.

Whence the devil says to himself about you: "Just as I had intended, they busy themselves with feasting and riotous living. But my eyes and ears and belly, and my very veins, are full of their froth, and my breasts, with their vices. For they refuse to labor for their God, and they consider Him nothing. Therefore, I will begin to wage war on them, and, by playing my games with them, I will lead them astray, since I do not find them laboring in the field of their Lord, as He commands them. O you, my disciples and followers, you have been punished publicly far more than they. And because this is so, rise up against them, strip away all their riches and honor, despoil and destroy them." Thus says the devil to himself, and in this way he will fulfill the judgment of God against many people. But I Who Am say to those who hear me: "When this time comes, ruin will fall upon you at the hands of certain people, you wicked sinners, and they will pursue you relentlessly, and they will not cover up your works, but will lay them bare, and they will say about you: These are scorpions in their morals and snakes in their works. Moreover, in their zeal toward the Lord, they will curse you, saying 'the way of the wicked shall perish' [Ps 1.6]. For they will mock your wicked ways and sneer at you."

But the people who will do this, themselves seduced by the devil and serving as his emissaries, will come with wan faces and, clothing themselves in sanctity, will ally themselves with great secular princes.[3] And they will say to them about you: "Why do you keep them with you and how can you stand to have them near you, when they are polluting the whole earth with their iniquity?"

The people who say these things about you will walk about in black robes, with proper tonsure, and will appear to men serene and peaceful in all their ways. Moreover, they do not love avarice, and do

---

3. That is, the Cathars.

not have money, and, in their secret selves, they hold abstinence as so great a virtue that they can scarcely be reproached. The devil, however, is within these men, revealing himself to them in the obscuring lightning, just as he was at the beginning of the world before his fall. And he makes himself, as it were, like the prophets, saying: "People foolishly imagine that I appear like rabid and unclean animals or come in the guise of flies, but, in reality, I fly on wings in the flashing thunder and deceive them so fully that they fulfill my will perfectly. In this way, I will make myself like the almighty God in the wonders I perform."

For the devil works through the spirits of the air, who, because of men's wicked deeds, buzz around in the air in countless hordes like the flies and gnats which plague people in the sweltering heat with their sheer numbers. For the devil deceives them in this way because he does not dissuade them from chastity, but indeed permits their desire to be chaste. Therefore, they do not love women, but flee from them. And thus they appear in public as if they were filled with sanctity, and say with mocking words: Before now, all other people who wanted to remain chaste burned themselves up like roast fish. But no pollution of the flesh or lust dares to touch us, because we are saintly and filled with the Holy Spirit.

Wake up! The misguided people of today have no idea what they are doing, no more than those who went before us in times past. For, at that time, others who err in the Catholic faith will fear them and will serve them slavishly, imitating them as much as possible. And when the full gamut of this error has been run, these people will everywhere persecute and exile the teachers and wise men who remain true to the Catholic faith—but not all of them, because some of them are mighty knights for God's justice. Moreover, they will not be able to affect certain congregations of saints, whose way of life is upright. For this reason, they advise princes and wealthy men to coerce teachers, wise men, and clerics with club and staff so that they may be made "just." And in some cases this will be accomplished, causing others to tremble with fear.

A SERMON

In the beginning of this their seduction into error, they will say to women: "It is not permitted for you to be with us, but because you do not have good and upright teachers, obey us and do whatever we say, whatever we command, and then you will be saved." And in this way they draw women to themselves and lead them into their own error. Therefore, they will say in the pride of their puffed-up spirit: "We are completely victorious."

But I Who Am say: "Thus the iniquity which will purge iniquity will fall upon your heads, just as it is written: 'He made darkness his covert, his pavilion round about him: dark waters in the clouds of the air'" [Ps 17.12]. And, because of your wicked deeds, which are devoid of light, God will wreak His vengeance upon you, and He will be so hidden in that vengeance that you will have no hope of deliverance. For no one will call out for mercy for you, but everybody will say that you are wicked. The law and doctrine are from heaven, and, if you were an ornament of virtue and a fragrant garden of delights, God should have been living in you through these.

But you are a bad example to others, since no rivulet of good reputation flows from you, so that, with respect to the soul, you have neither food to eat nor clothes to wear, but only unjust deeds without the good of knowledge. Therefore, your honor will perish and the crown will fall from your head. Thus injustice calls forth justice, and it seeks out and searches for every scandal, just as it is written: "For it must needs be that scandals come: but nevertheless woe to that man by whom the scandal cometh" [Matt 18.7]. Thus the wicked deeds of mankind must be purged through tribulation and contrition, and many woes are laid up for those also who, through their irreligious acts, bring misery upon others. These are people of no faith, seduced by the devil, and they will be the scourge to discipline you rigorously, because you do not worship God with pure hearts. And they will not cease to torment you until all your injustice and your iniquities are purged.

These, however, are not those deceivers who will come before the last great day when the devil has flown on high, just as he began to fight against God in the beginning, but these are their precursors. Nevertheless, after their perverse worship of Baal and their other depraved works are made known, princes and other great men will rush upon them, and will kill them like rabid wolves, wherever they can be found. Then the dawn of justice will arise, and your last days will be better than those before, and, on account of your past trials, you will be devout, and you will shine like pure gold, and thus you will remain through long ages.

At that time many people will be amazed that such mighty storms heralded this time of mercy. But those who lived before these times fought mightily against their desires to the great peril of their bodies, but they were unable to extricate themselves. In your times, however, you will be engaged in restless wars on account of your desires and your unsettled morals, and, through them, you will be reduced to nothing.

Whoever wishes to escape these dangers, therefore, let him beware lest with darkened eyes he run into the nets of these woes. But let each, to the best of his ability, escape them through good works and the safe harbor of uncorrupted will, and God will provide him with His aid.

Poor little timorous figure of a woman that I am, I have worn myself out for two whole years so that I might bring this message in person to the magistrates, teachers, and other wise men who hold the higher positions in the Church. But because the Church was divided,[4] I have kept quiet.

---

4. The schism began in 1159 when the cardinals elected two popes, Alexander III and Victor IV. Frederick Barbarossa gave his approval to the latter, and when Victor died in 1164, Frederick, in blatant defiance of the Church, elected his own pope, Paschal II, and, after him, another, Calixtus III. The schism lasted until 1177, when Frederick and Alexander III were reconciled.

The Provost Volmar

This letter is from Volmar, Hildegard's devoted secretary, close associate, friend, and it is a joy to hear his voice at last. It was he who was the "certain monk" that Hildegard referred to in her letter to Bernard of Clairvaux in 1147. The year is now 1170, and since we know that Volmar has served as her secretary and confidant at least since 1141, that means that he has been with her, her staunch supporter, for thirty years or more at this point. The letter is mainly concerned with a contemplation of the possible death of Hildegard and the terrible loss that will be to the Church, to the world—with Volmar being wholly unaware, of course, that he will be the first to go. For he died in 1173, some six years before Hildegard. So, instead, it was Hildegard who endured the loss, and she mourned for Volmar as one who had been orphaned.

Letter 58 ❧ from the Provost Volmar

To Hildegard, reverend lady, sweet mother, saintly mistress, truthful and approved confidante of God, in the convent at St. Rupert, Volmar her son, though unworthy, and the entire congregation of her maidens, along with all others who cling to her, and who serve God and St. Rupert, albeit lukewarmly. With due subjection, due obedience, and due filial affection, they offer their prayers that they may be consoled by the breasts of her consolation [cf. Is 66.11], so that they may become partakers of the heavenly country after the exile of this world.

Although, now, sweet mother, we are privileged to see you every day with fleshly eyes, and hear you with fleshly ears, and can cling to you daily (as is proper) and understand that the Holy Spirit speaks to us through you, we still have no doubt that at some time, as it pleases God, you will be taken away from us, and that, henceforth, we will no longer see you with our fleshly eyes, for there is no man that "shall live, and not see death" [Ps 88.49]. But this is a matter that we cannot even mention without tears.

When that time comes, our grief and woe will surpass the joy we now feel. Who then will give answers to all who seek to understand their condition? Who will provide fresh interpretations of the Scriptures? Who then will utter songs never heard before and give voice to that unheard language? Who will deliver new and unheard-of sermons on feast days? Who then will give revelations about the spirits of the departed? Who will offer revelations of things past, present, and future? Who will expound the nature of creation in all its diversity? We know that God's grace has bestowed these capacities upon you along with a sweet and humble character and a heart that pours out maternal affection on all around you.

O what divine mercy resides in His gifts! O how pointless are human anxieties! O "vanity of vanities" [Eccles 1.2]! Why do so many undertake difficult journeys into remote parts of the world to seek out the teachings of various men—and all in vain? Why, when afflicted with thirst, hunger, and cold, do they sweat over the profundity, or, rather, the enigma, of sententiae, listening to disputes in the courts and remaining awake at all hours of the night? We know for certain that they endure all these things not with a simple view to zeal, but out of the depravity of simony. Thus because they accomplish very little, if anything, they cannot grasp the commandment of the Spirit of God—nay, rather, they extinguish the spark of God's Spirit by their contempt for it, although they think that by that spark they are something important. The result is that to the embarrassment of modern scholastics who abuse the knowledge given them from above, the Spirit of prophecy and vision, revitalized in a fragile vessel and without help of secular learning, brings forth things that they cannot comprehend in any way. For the Spirit gives what instruction He will and "breatheth where he will" [John 3.8]. And so here we see the principle fulfilled that God, according to the Scripture, has chosen the foolish and weak things of this world in order to confound the wise and strong [cf. I Cor 1.27].

We say such things, sweet mother, not to put down your simple nature as if we were enflamed with the torch of envy for such a gift, a gift bestowed upon you that you might use it zealously. Nor do we speak this way so that we may boast vaingloriously, since we are the ones who are especially yours, who are with you most often, and who sedulously hear your voice. No, we do so in order to show that, compared with chaste goodness and piety, the determined exertions of such men[1] are not sufficient for investigating and comprehending the heights of true doctrine, for a teacher moves his lips, outwardly, in vain, unless, inwardly, the Spirit informs the hearts of those listening to him. In you, however, there are more signs of the virtues and more evidence of the miracles of God and the Holy Spirit than we could possibly say. Or want to say, for it is the task of others to praise you and spread your fame; it is ours to marvel at you, venerate you, and love you.

Because you know all this by your experience better than we, and because a few words are sufficient to understand many things, we refrain from saying more to the wise. We give thanks to God, for Whom all things are possible, Who gave you to us, and Who illumined you by His spirit for the glory of His name and for the salvation of many. We humbly and sincerely pray that He will bestow health of body and strength of mind upon you, so that He may abundantly spread His gift, which He has poured out upon you, for the edification of the whole Church.

Volmar, Hildegard's secretary and friend for some thirty years, died in 1173. He had also served as provost of Mount St. Rupert, attending to the spiritual affairs of the nuns, so that his death left the community bereft of spiritual guidance. When Hildegard petitioned Mount St. Disibod for the appointment of a new provost, the churlish Abbot Helengerus, with whom Hildegard had had other difficulties, refused to comply, blithely disregarding the agreement of some twenty-years' standing that the nuns of Mount St. Rupert were to have the right of election of the provost of their choice. As a result of this obstinacy, the vacancy remained for as long as a year, perhaps a year and a half, while Hildegard sought desperately for a remedy. As usual, the unshakeable Hildegard is not to be denied, and her following letter to Pope Alexander III finally achieves some results.

Letter 59 to Pope Alexander III

O lofty and glorious one, first appointed through the Word of God through Whom every creature, rational and non-rational, was made according to its kind, to you has that same Word, by robing Himself in humanity, specially yielded the keys of the kingdom of heaven, that is, the power of binding and loosing [cf. Matt 16.19].

You are also, O most excellent father, the source of all spiritual offices. Some of these sound the trumpet of God's justice in the Church, which shines because it has been clothed with various ornaments, while others set good examples for other people by imitating the lives of the saints, and if they bring forth good works, they attribute them to God and not to themselves. Rejoicing in those who seek to emulate them, they follow the saints who conquered their flesh and, fighting against the sins of the devil, fortified themselves with the clear victory of heaven's army, and with good will looked upon God, just as the angels do.

And so, O mild father, imitate that kindly father who joyfully received his penitent son at his return and killed the fatted calf for his sake [cf. Luke 15.20ff]; and emulate also that man who washed with wine the wounds of the one beaten by robbers [cf. Luke 10.30ff]. By these examples understand the harshness of reproof and the godliness of compassion. And be the Morning Star which precedes the sun, a guide to the Church, which, for far too long, has been lacking in the light of God's justice because of the dense cloud of schism. And with God's zeal seize the penitents and anoint them with the oil of mercy, because God desires mercy more than sacrifice [Hosea 6.6; Matt 9.13, 12.7].

Now O gentlest father, my sisters and I bend our knees before your paternal piety, praying that you deign to regard the poverty of this poor little woman. We are in great distress because the abbot of Mount St. Disibod and his brothers have taken away our privileges and the right of election which we have always had, rights which we have been ever careful to retain. For if they will not grant us reverential and religious men, such as we seek, spiritual religion will be totally destroyed among us. Therefore, my lord, for God's sake, help us, so that we may retain the man we have elected to that office. Or, if not, let us seek out and receive others, where we can, who will look after us in accordance with the will of God and our own needs.

Now again we ask you, most pious father, not to despise our petition or our messengers, who on the advice of our faithful friend took up our cause. May you grant that which they seek to obtain from you, so that after the end of this life, which is already hastening toward evening, you may come to that inextinguishable light and hear the sweet voice of the Lord saying, "Well done, good and faithful servant, because thou hast been faithful over a few things, I will place thee over many things: enter thou into the joy of thy lord" [Matt 25.21, 23]. Incline the ears of your piety to our supplications, therefore, and be the bright day to us and to them, so that from the kindness of your generosity we may give thanks to the Lord together, and you may rejoice forever in eternal happiness.

In answer to Hildegard's request, the pope appoints Wezelinus, abbot of St. Andrew in Cologne, who just happens to be Hildegard's nephew, to attend to the matter. Wezelinus acquitted himself well in this disagreeable task, for through his efforts, Helengerus assigned the monk Gottfried to Hildegard to serve as provost and secretary. A secondary benefit—to the community and to posterity—came out of this appointment, for Gottfried took the occasion to write a biography of Hildegard, though he unfortunately died before bringing it to conclusion.

Letter 60 ⁌ *from Pope Alexander III*

Alexander, servant of the servants of God, to our beloved son, abbot of St. Andrew in Cologne, greetings and apostolic blessings.

On behalf of our beloved daughter in Christ, Hildegard, prioress of Mount St. Rupert in Bingen and of the sisters of that place, you should know that it has come to our attention that when, according to their custom, they had elected for themselves a master and provost from the monastery of St. Disibod, the abbot of that place was unwilling to acknowledge the election of the person from his monastery, and even up to the present time still refuses to assign that person to them. Wherefore since it is proper that there be provision for the aforementioned sisters in those things which pertain to the salvation of their souls, we mandate to your discretion through apostolic writings that you call together both sides to your presence once you have made inquiry into this and have more clearly understood this matter of the election of the provost. Then decide the case with proper justice. And if these sisters cannot have a provost from that monastery, see to it, at least, that they have a competent one from another.

Miscellaneous Letters and Visions

Hildegard has somehow become aware of a religious zealot, who has an abundance of pious fervor, but very little of what she considers proper discipline and balance, for moderation in religious matters is one of Hildegard's cardinal principles. Taking compassion on the man, Hildegard writes an abbot friend begging him to take the man in and subject him to a reasonable regimen.

Letter 61 ❧ to an Abbot

O venerable father, you who for the love of God have set me in the bosom of your compassion, I beg you for the love of God to give heed to me, unworthy handmaiden of God that I am. Specifically, I ask you to receive with paternal compassion this penitent individual, who, on account of his sins, desires to become a monk. I beseech you to give him good counsel so that he does not weaken his body through irrational fasting and die from lack of sustenance.

Impose a moderate penance upon him so that he may—with discretion—overcome the devil, who is trying to deceive him. For discretion is the mother of the virtues, and she rules and regulates them all. Do this so that he may be pleasing to God, for the ancient serpent encourages overzealous fasting so that he may deceive and gulp down the person who longs for virtue but is lacking in discretion. Therefore, present this sheep to almighty God for the love of Him Who left the ninety sheep behind and placed the one on His shoulders [cf. Matt 18.12–13; Luke 15.4–5]. Do this for the forgiveness of all the sins of omission you have been guilty of throughout your life.

I hope in God that your gaze will be like the blazing sun, that you will be the faithful servant of God, and that you will live in His presence forever.

The emphasis in this letter on her own feminine ignorance and her fear of instructing her (male) superiors, along with the stress on the "true vision," indicates, surely, the difficulty of the message about to be proclaimed. Hildegard seeks a measure of tolerance for those of a different faith, apparently here a group of Jewish women who have caught her attention. Not absolute tolerance, of course, not in this age: They are ignorant of the true Faith; they are benighted. Teach them, but do not abuse them. Reading further between the lines, one senses that the letter is directed at a specific instance of harsh intolerance.

Letter 62 to a Teacher

O teacher, you have been thoroughly imbued with the teachings of the Scriptures. Now, may God, the Creator of the world, fill you with a thirst for works of righteousness, and may the Living Fountain illumine you, inebriating you with good and saintly purpose from the torrent of His pleasure [cf. Ps 35.9] so that in the light of the Father you may see light [cf. Ps 35.10], and, by seeing, be eternally satisfied, like the angels, who desire nothing more than to gaze upon Him.

I, a poor little form of a woman, obey the teaching of my superiors. But I scarcely know the rudiments of learning, and I am terribly afraid to speak or write to my male superiors about those things which I see in my spirit in the True Light, in my spirit only, unaided by my corporeal eyes. Nevertheless, I say to you—because I have seen it in a true vision—that those women are like the people under the Old Law, under which dispensation the root of the Righteous One existed, but remained almost withered because they did not know the teaching of the Son of God, which they themselves had proclaimed in their prophecy. Thus those women indeed know faith, but, living in the fatness of carnal desire, they do not yet fully perform the works of faith. Let them call frequently upon God in bitterness of heart, but let them also be told that those who are under the Old Law follow the letter, which kills, not the Spirit, which gives life [cf. II Cor 3.6]. Let them be taught this, lest they worship God by faith alone, which, without works, is dead [cf. James 2.26].

Therefore, warn these women to abandon the wicked way of their sins, which is fed by a deadly sort of apathy, and instruct them to hasten to the fountain of righteousness, just as a hart runs to the fountain of waters [cf. Ps 41.2]. For they delight in the taste of their sins, just as they delight in the taste of food. Teach them to take refuge in an upright way of life, and, like the one who sold all he had and bought the one pearl of great price [cf. Matt 13.46], to gird themselves for spiritual service in order to gain eternal life, by abandoning that way of life they now observe, through which they cannot be saved.

O master, may God make you a mirror of holiness, so that you may remain with Him blissfully forever.

This document is listed in the standard edition of the correspondence as number 376. Yet it is not actually a letter, but an isolated prose piece, a portion of a letter at one time perhaps, describing Hildegard's vision of the torments of purgatory. Since, however, Hildegard is so frequently asked about the fate of departed souls, it seems appropriate to include it here.

Letter 63 ❧ *Vision of a Soul in Purgatory*

In a vision of my waking soul, I saw the following things about a certain soul: When that soul had left its body, it was adjudged by the highest Judge, in accordance with the merits of its works, to be sent into an arid region, and this region was like land that had been beaten upon by torrential rains and then dried up and creased, as it were, by great ridges because of an intemperate climate. For this land was turned to the North, and seemingly at the very walls of the North I saw a kind of building that looked like a house, but I could not tell what was in it. Then, I saw venomous scorpions coming from the South, and from the East rushed horrible wild boars gnashing their teeth and bellowing with a mighty roar.

This soul was whirled about, here and there, by a huge whirlwind, and blown around in the midst of a great abundance of straw, flying like thatch torn from a roof and destroyed.[1] After it had been worn out in this way by the whirlwind, it was thrown into that house I mentioned before and, there, it was subjected to such fierce fire that it glowed like red-hot iron. Then, it was thrown among the poisonous scorpions, which punctured it with their venom, and, afterward, among the wild boars, which took great bites out of it. Thus on account of its instability and its false and deceiving way of life, this soul suffered the afflictions of the whirlwind, in company with that straw, and on account of certain hidden sins, which were very grievous, it was tortured by the fire in that house, and on account of its continually duplicitous tongue, it suffered the poison of the scorpions, and on account of its raping (as I learned in the true vision), it was torn among the boars.

---

1. The straw may appear strange here, but Hildegard in the *Scivias* (prol III.7) provides a proper explanation. There, she describes the column of the Trinity, to the southwest side of which appear heaps of dry straw, and, later, explains that the straw stands for those who negate and reject the Catholic faith.

I also saw and learned, however, that there was a door closed off in the North so that that soul would never fall into the infernal pit, because, while living in the body, it had been disciplined by its superiors in accordance with the Rule, and, by God, through physical infirmity. But I learned that it would suffer these punishments for a long, long time, for it had sinned for a very long time.

This document, listed as number 369 in the standard edition of the letters, is not actually a letter, but a recounting of one of Hildegard's visions. But since this vision of a swaggering, self-important religious zealot so vividly illustrates her reaction to the people of her time—as well as her ultimately merciful spirit—it merits inclusion here.

Letter 64 ❧ *A Vision of the Soul of a Certain Sinner*

In a true vision, I saw certain people sinning in their abundance, others out of their own foolishness, and still others because of impiety. Among the impious, I saw a certain man who behaved in very wild and savage ways, and I saw that sometimes he shouted and threw himself about, and did whatever he pleased, and that sometimes, to gratify his own spirit, he followed his own will in his prayers and service to God. And I saw that he looked wholly to himself without even the slightest nod to that ascent that leads to God, raging in his frenzy at other people.

Therefore, the devil caused sinful spirits to enter into him like the sighing of the wind, and they persuaded him that he could perform miracles, but because of his bitter spirit he wouldn't tell anybody about his new powers. And so in the turmoil of his mind, he sought out a forest and wanted to go there in order to perform his miracles, acts beyond the capacity of mankind. And in this desire to reach that forest, he attempted to walk on water and there perform miracles. But seeing this and knowing what he was up to, the devil roiled up the waters, and the man, in his futile attempts to escape, plunged headlong to his death. He hated to die in this way, and he remembered in bitter penitence that the devil had deceived him. And so as he died, he cried out, "Lord, help me" [cf. Ps 108.26]. He would gladly have lived, but he died nonetheless.

Now, I know that his soul is enveloped in so intense a blackness that I cannot attempt to describe it—but not in the blackness of the pit of hell, which will never end. Therefore, I see the bright essence of the good deeds that he did shining in the South, and this causes the devil to blush. Nevertheless, his soul is not now a part of that bright essence. But, poor little woman that I am, I heard and saw in the anguish of my soul that in the fulness of time, when all the works of man will be brought to perfection in the just judgment of God, this man's soul will not be damned, because at the very end he said "I repent."

Now let all the faithful hear these words and flee from this sin so that they do not trust wholly to themselves as if their will were God, because they are not complete in themselves, but they must look to Him Who is their God, and then they will recognize that it was because the man in the parable above looked wholly to himself that he found nothing.

This graphic, peculiarly Hildegardian depiction of the Fall, is too good to miss, even if it is not precisely a "letter."

Letter 65   *Satan's Rape of the First Woman*

And again, under the altar which stands before the eyes of God [cf. Apoc 6.9], and under the throne of God, I saw a shining white multitude [cf. Apoc 7.9], and I heard them saying: O throng of Israelites, you who belong to our company because you abandoned the world and bore the yoke of the Lord [cf. Matt 11.29], hear these words: When the ancient serpent uttered his deceptive words to the first woman [cf. Gen 3.1ff], and she did not resist his counsel, that serpent caused the foulest, most disgusting penis to issue forth from

MISCELLANEOUS LETTERS AND VISIONS

his mouth, in such a way that she swallowed it into her womb. From this, death came forth, and it cast a shadow over the light of mystical generation that God had created in Adam and Eve, so that, afterward, that light appeared no more. And the serpent was fully aware that the world was not supposed to die out, but he knew also that, henceforth, mankind would be born sexually through that penis of his shame.[2]

Therefore, when a man succumbs to his base instincts and fulfills all his desire in that penis of his, that serpent spews black fire from his mouth, which, afterward, becomes the torment of such pleasure. Then, the whole diabolical gang looks at that fire and mocks the man, laughing and saying, "Where is that man's God now?" Yet those who do not succumb but achieve victory over their desires prepare arrows in the quiver [cf. Ps 10.3] and shoot them with luminous fire at the serpent's penis, puncturing it with wounds in such a way that the serpent is shamed, like a man who knows that he is naked, but cannot cover himself. Then, like a roaring lion—in the schisms of heretics and in the filth and shame of every kind of evil—he sharpens all his strength against those wounds so as to hide them somehow.

Now, all you faithful within the chancel of the Church, hear and understand so that you may obtain victory over the devil's wiles, and avoid destroying the honor and bliss of your happiness—and so that we who stand beneath the altar and the throne of God may rejoice with you, for we rejoice when you expel the devil from yourselves through good works.

This letter from Ludwig of St. Eucharius, a close friend and confidant of Hildegard's, provides eloquent testimony of her well-established reputation as prophet and seer. It was to Ludwig that Hildegard turned for assistance

---

2. Barbara Newman, in personal correspondence, calls this the devil's "only half-metaphorical rape of Eve." We would also like to thank Professor Newman for her assistance with this problematic letter.

in finding a replacement for Volmar, and, later, after Hildegard's death, it was Ludwig who commissioned Theodoric to finish the Life of Hildegard left incomplete at the death of Gottfried.

Letter 66 from Ludwig, Abbot of St. Eucharius

To the holy virgin dedicated to God, Hildegard, his beloved mother, Ludwig, abbot in name only of St. Eucharius, greetings. My affection for you is so great that nobody except me could fully understand it.

How ludicrous it would be for butterflies to greet eagles in a letter; or fleas, harts; or worms, lions. Just so, it would be strange, even laughable for me, a sinner, who has little, if any, capacity in any divine or human skill, to presume to write you. For adorned with the miraculous privilege of chastity, you have been endowed by God with such lofty and remarkable sagacity that you surpass the insight not only of modern philosophers and logicians, but even the prophets of old.

And yet with your customary kindness, saintly mother, you will surely not deny pardon to my rash presumption, for our friendship has made me bold to write to you again. And I will not be deterred from writing you or coming to see you frequently by the hardship of the road, for the benefit obtained from hearing you is all the more to be desired the greater the effort it requires to do so. For we possess those things more gratefully that we acquire by exertion.

Therefore, my lady, do not let our wickedness distress you, for compassionate love will lend you the strength which your physical infirmity denies you. I greatly long for the letter you promised to send me. So please do not delay sending it by the present messenger. I pray you to write back what seems to you best regarding the matter entrusted to you.

During the course of her reply to Ludwig, Hildegard laments her bereft condition at the death of her devoted secretary and friend, Volmar. And since Volmar was her untiring assistant in her writing, Hildegard requests Ludwig to stand in his stead by *"correcting"* (that is, acting, in effect, as copyeditor of) her latest work.

Letter 67 ❧ to Ludwig, Abbot of St. Eucharius

In regard to your request I looked to the true vision I see in my soul, and I saw and heard these words: "You were chosen to govern that church with the rod of chastisement, an election not improper in the sight of God. Therefore, labor in that church to the best of your ability with God's help, for God's justice has grown cold among many who run on the narrow path of spiritual life, because they long to follow their own will. This time will not show you the perfection of holiness that the Holy Spirit first planted in that community. Therefore, restrain yourself, lest, led astray by the esteem acquired by an honorable name or by secular inclination, you fall short of the stability of your good intentions."

Imitate the gentlest Father in humility, patience, and mercy so that you will deserve to hear Him say to you for your good labors, "Well done, good servant" [Matt 25.21ff], and so that you may live blissfully in eternal beatitude. I and all my sisters zealously commend to God the infirmity of your body and all the pressure brought to bear on your heart. Therefore, fear not, because God, by Whose grace you are endowed with wisdom and knowledge, will never abandon you.

Gentle father, I give thanks to God, and to you, because you deigned to sympathize with me, a poor little form of a woman, in my infirmity and pain. Now, like an orphan I toil alone to do God's work, because my helper has been taken away from me, as it pleased God. The book which I wrote with his help through the grace of the Holy Spirit according to a true vision is not yet finished. As soon as it is completely written, I will offer it to you for correction.

This letter appears to be a follow-up to the preceding one, in which Hildegard had indicated to Ludwig that she would send her book to him for correction. That volume, the Book of Divine Works, is now complete, and this is, apparently, the cover letter transmitted with the copy of that last major work.

Letter 68   to Ludwig, Abbot of St. Eucharius

The sun rises in the morning, and from its appointed place it suffuses all the clouds with its light like a mirror, and it rules and illumines all creatures with its warmth until evening. Just so, did God fashion all creation—which is mankind—and, afterward, vivified it with the breath of life and illumined it.

Just as morning first arises with damp cold and shifting clouds, so also man in his infancy is damp and cold, because his flesh is growing and his bones are not yet full of marrow, and his blood does not have its full vigor. As the third hour begins to grow warm with the course of the sun, so also man begins to chew his food, and learns to walk.

In his youth when infancy is over, man, becoming bold, happy, and carefree, begins to think of what he will do in life. If in the light of the sun he chooses the good by turning to the right, he will become fruitful in good works. But if he turns to the left to pursue evil, he will become black and corrupt in the evil of sin. When he reaches the ninth hour while doing his work, he becomes arid and weary in his flesh and marrow and the other powers through which he earlier grew and advanced. So also the great Artisan set in order the ages of the world from the first hour until the evening.

Therefore, O father, you who take your name from the Father, reflect on how you began and how the course of your life has proceeded, for in your infancy you lacked wisdom, and in your youth you were happy and carefree. In the meantime, however, you were seeking the affairs of the unicorn, all unbeknownst to yourself.[3] This is the subject of my writing, which resonates of the fleshly garment of the Son of God, Who loved a virginal nature and rested in the lap of the Virgin like the unicorn, and with the sweetest sound of beautiful faith gathered all the Church unto Himself.

Be mindful, O faithful father, what you have often heard of that aforesaid garment of the Son of God from this poor weak form of a woman. Now, because the almighty Judge has taken my helper from me, I submit my writing to you, humbly asking you to preserve it carefully and correct it diligently. Then, your name will be inscribed in the book of life. In this you will imitate the blessed Gregory, who, despite the burden he bore as bishop of Rome, never ceased from his writing, which was infused with the sound of the lyre of the Holy Spirit.

Now, put on the armor of heaven like a valiant knight, and wash away the deeds of your foolish youth. In the angelic vestment of the monk's habit, labor strenuously at noon, before the day ends, so that you will be received joyfully into the company of angels in the heavenly tabernacles.

This piece was written sometime between 1173 and 1179. It is not a letter, but it does seem to be highly personal. Is this the one time when Hildegard expresses something of self-doubt? Or perhaps it is simply an exhortation, in the usual medieval commonplace, directed to herself, to avoid pride in her great gift. In any case, the reference to the Living Light seems pointed directly at Hildegard herself.

Letter 69 ෴ *a Message*

God is inconceivable and invisible. No one has the capacity to know or grasp His hidden mysteries. Through the first deception, the devil,

---

3. The point of this rather obscure phrase is, apparently, that the person was seeking God even before he himself was aware of it.

by his serpentine guile, did great harm to that which was celestial in man, but God wanted to salvage that new thing.

It often happens thus when some inspiration comes forth from the Living Light, which is God, touching a person's spirit: If that person glories in it in a way other than he should, or if he climbs higher than he has the ability to do, the serpent laughs scornfully to himself about such a fool. Therefore, let those things which proceed from the truth be heard, and those things which come from lies be, mercifully, cast away, for no one has reached such perfection that he is not a liar in some way or other, just as David, inspired by the Holy Spirit, says, "Every man is a liar" [Ps 115.11].

Guibert of Gembloux

In 1175 Hildegard received a letter from the man, a monk of Gembloux, who was to become her last intimate associate and secretary. Having read her works and having reflected, as he says, upon the gifts bestowed upon her by the Holy Spirit, "gifts scarcely heard of through all the ages up to the present day," he writes in burning curiosity, seeking answers to certain questions he has about her divine inspiration: Does she give voice to her visions in German while someone else takes them down in Latin? Does she, "as is commonly said," forget her visions as soon as they are written down? Is she learned, or does her wisdom come wholly through inspiration? When Hildegard failed to answer this first letter, he wrote again, adding further questions: Does she receive her visions in dreams while asleep, or do they come in a state of ecstasy? Are her nuns' crowns dictated by divine inspiration, or are they merely for feminine ornamentation? Does the title of her book Scivias mean "Knowing the Ways," or is there a better translation? Has she written other books? Guibert becomes totally absorbed in his fascination with Hildegard and stubbornly insistent on answers to his questions. He was to write her in all some eight long and rather garrulous letters, letters filled with other questions that he kept pressing her to answer. Guibert was a persistent and dogged sort of monk! The following letter is Hildegard's long and quite detailed answers to most, though not all, of the

questions posed in Guibert's first two. The letter is very informative, giving details that we get nowhere else. Although, for instance, Hildegard refers constantly to the Living Light in all her writing, here, for the first and only time, we hear of a Shadow of the Living Light. The letter is too good to miss, an intimate and delightful portrait of the woman who in the grip of her divine inspiration forgets all her sorrow and pain and becomes "more like a young girl than an old woman."

Letter 70 🙵 to Guibert of Gembloux

The words I speak are not my own, nor any human being's. I merely report those things I received in a supernal vision. O servant of God, you gaze into the mirror of faith in order to know God, and through the formation of man in whom God established and sealed His miracles, you have become a son of God. For just as a mirror, which reflects all things, is set in its own container, so too the rational soul is placed in the fragile container of the body. In this way, the body is governed in its earthly life by the soul, and the soul contemplates heavenly things through faith. Hear, then, O son of God, what the unfailing Light says.

Man is both heavenly and earthly [cf. I Cor 15.47–49]: through the good knowledge of the rational soul, he is heavenly; and through the bad, fragile and full of darkness. And the more he recognizes the good in himself, the more he loves God. For if someone looks in a mirror and finds that his face is very dirty, he will want to wash it clean. So too, if he understands that he has sinned and been caught up in vain pursuits, let him groan and cry out with the Psalmist because his good knowledge makes him aware that he is polluted: "O daughter of Babylon, miserable" [Ps 136.8]. Here is the sense of this verse: human desire was tainted through the poison of the serpent. Thus it is impoverished and wretched, for despite the fact that it tastes the glory of eternal life through its good knowledge, it nevertheless fails to seek that glory from God with true desire—for which reason it has a low reputation in philosophical thought. But blessed is he who understands that he has his life from God, and blessed is he whose knowledge teaches him that God created and redeemed him. For through this divinely given freedom, he breaks the evil habit of his sins, and poor as he is in celestial riches, he dashes his wretchedness upon the rock which is the foundation of beatitude. For when a person knows that he is filthy and cannot resist tasting sin whatsoever, black birds completely befoul him. But then also the rational soul, which he neither sees nor knows, leads him to put his faith in God by believing. Yet although he knows that this is his nature, and knows too that he will live forever, he still cannot keep himself from sinning over and over again. And so: O how lamentable is the fact that God makes such fragile vessels which cannot refrain from sin, save through the grace of God. And yet how wondrous that these same vessels are sometimes adorned with the stars of His miracles. For even Peter, who vowed vehemently that he would never deny the Son of God, was himself not safe [cf. Matt 26.33ff; Mark 14.29ff; Luke 22.33ff; John 13.37f]. The same was true of many other saints, who fell in their sins. Yet these were all, afterward, made more useful and more perfect than they would have been if they had not fallen.

O faithful servant, I—poor little woman that I am—say these words to you again in a true vision: If God were to raise my body as He does my spirit in this vision, my mind and heart would still not be free from fear, because, although I have been cloistered from childhood, I am fully aware that I am only human. For many wise men have been so miraculously inspired that they revealed many mysteries, and yet they fell, because in their vanity they ascribed all these miracles to their own power. On the other hand, those who have drunk deeply of God's wisdom in elevation of spirit while still regarding themselves as nothing—these have become the pillars of heaven. Paul was such a one, for although he was a far better preacher than all the other disciples, he still counted himself as nothing [cf. II Cor 12.11].

Likewise, the evangelist John was mild and humble, and therefore drank deeply of divine revelations [cf. Apoc 1.1–2].

And how could God work through me if I were not aware that I am but a poor little creature? God works His will for the glory of His name, not for the glory of any earthly person. Indeed I always tremble in fear, since I know that I cannot safely rely on my own innate capacity. But I stretch out my hands to God so that He might raise me up like a feather, which, having no weight of its own, flies on the wind. Still, I cannot fully understand those things I see, as long as I am an invisible spirit in a fleshly body, because man was injured in both these faculties.

I am now more than seventy years old. But even in my infancy, before my bones, muscles, and veins had reached their full strength, I was possessed of this visionary gift in my soul, and it abides with me still up to the present day. In these visions my spirit rises, as God wills, to the heights of heaven and into the shifting winds, and it ranges among various peoples, even those very far away. And since I see in such a fashion, my perception of things depends on the shifting of the clouds and other elements of creation. Still, I do not hear these things with bodily ears, nor do I perceive them with the cogitations of my heart or the evidence of my five senses. I see them only in my spirit, with my eyes wide open, and thus I never suffer the defect of ecstasy in these visions. And, fully awake, I continue to see them day and night. Yet my body suffers ceaselessly, and I am racked by such terrible pains that I am brought almost to the point of death. So far, however, God has sustained me.

The light that I see is not local and confined. It is far brighter than a lucent cloud through which the sun shines. And I can discern neither its height nor its length nor its breadth. This light I have named "the shadow of the Living Light," and just as the sun and moon and stars are reflected in water, so too are writings, words, virtues, and deeds of men reflected back to me from it.

Whatever I see or learn in this vision I retain for a long period of time, and store it away in my memory. And my seeing, hearing, and knowing are simultaneous, so that I learn and know at the same instant. But I have no knowledge of anything I do not see there, because I am unlearned. Thus the things I write are those that I see and hear in my vision, with no words of my own added. And these are expressed in unpolished Latin, for that is the way I hear them in my vision, since I am not taught in the vision to write the way philosophers do. Moreover, the words I see and hear in the vision are not like the words of human speech, but are like a blazing flame and a cloud that moves through clear air. I can by no means grasp the form of this light, any more than I can stare fully into the sun.

And sometimes, though not often, I see another light in that light, and this I have called "the Living Light." But I am even less able to explain how I see this light than I am the other one. Suffice it to say that when I do see it, all my sorrow and pain vanish from my memory and I become more like a young girl than an old woman.

But the constant infirmity I suffer sometimes makes me too weary to communicate the words and visions shown to me, but nevertheless when my spirit sees and tastes them, I am so transformed, as I said before, that I consign all my sorrow and tribulation to oblivion. And my spirit drinks up those things I see and hear in that vision, as from an inexhaustible fountain, which remains ever full.

Moreover, that first light I mentioned, the one called "the shadow of the Living Light" is always present to my spirit. And it has the appearance of the vault of heaven in a bright cloud on a starless night. In this light I see those things I frequently speak of, and from its brightness I hear the responses I give to those who make inquiry of me.

In a vision I also saw that my first book of visions was to be called *Scivias*, for it was brought forth by way of the Living Light and not through any human instruction. I also had a vision about crowns. I saw that all the orders of the church have distinct emblems according to their celestial brightness, but that virginity has no such distinguishing emblem save the black veil and the sign of the cross. And I saw that a white veil to cover a virgin's head was to be the proper emblem of virginity. For this veil stands for the white garment which man once had, but subsequently lost, in Paradise. Furthermore, upon the virgin's head is to be set a circlet of three colors joined into one. For this circlet stands for the Holy Trinity. To this circlet four others are to be joined: the front bearing the Lamb of God; the right, a cherubim;[1] the left, an angel; and the one behind, man. For all of these are pendants to the Trinity. This sign given by God will bless God, for He once clothed the first man in the whiteness of light. All of this is fully described in the *Scivias*. And I wrote this *Scivias*, as well as other volumes, according to a true vision, and I continue my writing up to the present day.

Body and soul, I am totally ignorant, and I count myself as nothing. But I look to the living God and relinquish all these matters to Him, so that He, Who has neither beginning nor end, may preserve me from evil. And so pray for me, you who seek these words of mine, and all of you who long to hear them in faith—pray for me that I may remain God's servant in true happiness.

O child of God, you who faithfully seek salvation from the Lord, observe the eagle flying toward the clouds on two wings. If one of those wings is wounded, the eagle falls to earth and cannot rise, no matter how hard it tries. So too man flies with the two wings of rationality, that is to say, with the knowledge of good and evil. The right wing is good knowledge, and the left, evil. Evil knowledge serves the good, and good knowledge is kept in check by the evil, and is even made more discerning by it. Indeed the good is made wise in all things through the evil.

---

1. The plural *cherubim* used for the singular is a common medieval error.

Now, dear son of God, may the Lord raise the wings of your knowledge to straight paths so that although you come into contact with sin through the senses—since man's very nature makes it impossible not to sin—you nonetheless never willingly consent to sin. The heavenly choir sings praises to God for the person who acts in this way, because, although made from ashes, he loves God so much that, for His sake, he does not spare himself, but, totally despising the self, preserves himself from sinful works. O noble knight, be so valiant in the battle that you may take your place in the heavenly choir, so that God will say to you: "You are one of the sons of Israel, because in your great desire for heaven you direct the eyes of your mind to the lofty mountain."

As for all those you called my attention to in your letter, may they be guided by the Holy Spirit and inscribed in the Book of Life [cf. Apoc 20.12]. Moreover, O faithful servant of God, speak specifically to Lord Siger, and warn him not to turn from the right hand to the left [cf. Deut 5.32]. For if someone resists a vow that he has made, let him put on the breastplate of faith and the helmet of celestial desire [cf. Eph 6.14ff], and fight manfully. Then, he will successfully complete his journey. And let him consider the fact that when the first man obeyed the voice of his wife rather than the voice of God, he perished in his presumption [cf. Gen 3.17], because he consented to her. But if the tribulation appears to exceed their powers, let them remember the Scripture: "God is faithful, who will not suffer you to be tempted above that which you are able: but will make also with temptation issue, that you may be able to bear it" [I Cor 10.13]. Thus strengthened by this blessed promise, let him and his wife be of one mind, and let them follow whatever course of action is best, whether suggested by the husband or the wife. And let them not fall prey to that first deception, with the man accusing the woman, and the woman, the man. But let them settle this whole matter according to the will of God. I pray that the fire of the Holy Spirit so enkindle their hearts that they never withdraw from Him.

The following letter from the loquacious Guibert of Gembloux was included here with some little hesitation since it is so long, rambling, and discursive. Yet no one knows Hildegard better than Guibert, and no other letter supplies such detailed information about the enthusiastic acceptance of her as an inspired prophet of God by such a wide range of people. One has to make exception, of course, for the unrestrained enthusiasm of the excitable Guibert, but the picture he paints of the ardent reception by the assembled crowd has the ring of truth. Guibert is, to be sure, a fawning sort of personage, and gullible, one should probably add, but with the proper allowances being made he is worthy of our respect.

Letter 71 from Guibert of Gembloux

To the lady and mother, Hildegard, whom I will always receive with the most sincere affection, Guibert, her servant, with a prayer that she obtain lasting health of body and soul from the God of our salvation [cf. Ps 67.20].

In the first letter which I sent to you, blessed and worthy lady, I asked certain questions and made some personal observations, and thus quite naturally looked forward to a written response from you. In that letter, I also declared, unequivocally, that I had no hope of being able to come to see you—which, most certainly, I would not have done, if, at that time, I had had any notion or intention of seeking you out, lest my own words should convict me of trifling or of untrustworthiness. Still, I know—I am indeed certain—that things impossible for human beings are nonetheless possible with God [cf. Matt 19.26; Mark 10.27; Luke 18.27], to Whom immediately, whenever He wishes, things are possible [cf. Wisdom 12.18].

Moreover, I uttered those words of hesitation not out of any distrust of divine assistance (for it often gives comfort even to the ignorant), but because I am still uncertain whether it would be good for me to make this journey. For experience has taught me very well that God, in His great mercy, has frequently thwarted the ill-considered impulses of my foolish will. Yet, on the other hand, by bringing certain arguments to bear, He has quickened the slothfulness of my soul and recalled me to better things, even when I was striving in precisely the opposite direction. And it is this latter, revered mother—I confess in my great joy—that has happened to me by His grace and by your merits. For although I was doing nothing about seeking you out, or even thinking about it, He, Who, in the abundance of His mercy, exceeds the desires and merits of our prayers, and sometimes even adds what our prayers do not presume to ask, He, I believe, planted the resolve in me and enkindled the desire, when an opportunity and means of visiting you came our way. And He did this, I believe, because He knew that it would be good for me.

Hear briefly the upshot of these matters. Our mutual friend, Lord Siger, a man of notable family, all the more notable for his very clear devotion to God, had delivered my second letter to you, and, having returned from your presence, saintly lady, had been home scarcely a single night before sending word to me. For, behold, the very next morning, he sent a horse for me by a young man I knew well, and summoned me into his presence. And although I did not find him at home when I arrived, his wife, Elizabeth, herself a very fervent worshipper of God, gave me the letter you had sent me through him, sweet lady, and I received it with reverence and joy. Suspecting that the letter contained something remarkable and magnificent (as indeed turned out to be true), I did not dare to read it until I had prayed. Indeed—if I may reveal the complete agitation of my soul—I was terribly afraid that divine wrath, angered at my sins, would pour some kind of destruction upon me through your mouth immediately, or would at least threaten it for the future.

Therefore, I entered the church next to the house and placed your letter upon the altar. Then, falling to my knees, I prayed the Holy Spirit to make me worthy to read it and to so strengthen the weakness of my heart that I could accept what I would read.

Moreover, if any danger lay in store on account of my sins, I asked Him to show me a way to avert it through the prayers of the saints. Then I took up your letter again and read it two or three times in silence. And in sheer wonder at the words, I was, as it were, completely changed and brought almost into ecstasy, for the things said there surpassed my poor powers, and seemed to be more the voice of the Spirit or the speech of angels than of a human being. And so from the bottom of my heart, I blessed the Father of lights [cf. James 1.17], Who spoke and caused light to shine in the darkness [cf. Gen 1.3ff], and Who has filled your spirit with such great brightness that (as you unerringly note in this letter) you are inundated with a double light, ineffable and unending. One of these is with you constantly, that is to say with no intervening fluctuation; the other, only at certain times. Truly, by a special privilege among the women of our time, the light of God's visage has been sealed upon you [cf. Ps 4.7], in order that He might diffuse a salvific joy in your heart.

Truly, in this respect, my lady, your glory is unique! Unique, excepting always, of course, that eminent woman from whom the Sun of Righteousness arose [cf. Mal 4.2], He Who in the radiance of the holy ones was born from the womb of the Father before Lucifer. As the mother of such a one, that woman is rightly called the gate of perpetual light and the resplendent star of the sea. With the exception of her, I say, no other woman in the history of the world save you has ever brought it about that the female sex, which brought the darkness of death into the world, has been marked with the privilege of a greater gift or suffused with such great brightness.

Moreover, I poured out my thanks to our munificent Savior for that other gift, bestowed on you by heaven, for He has poured such grace forth upon your lips that, irrigated in certain parts by the distillation of your words and doctrine, the soil of the Church rejoices, putting forth shoots and producing worthy fruit, through God's kindness. And so let the Church sing a hymn to His name for this voluntary rain which God set apart for His heritage, for He has so magnified your name that your praise will never cease from the lips of men.

Finally, I am very grateful to you, sweet lady, commending you to God. For I have been granted my highest desire, since, as I gather from your words, you have deigned to give me a high place among your special friends, unworthy and undeserving though I am. Thus when you unlocked the chapel of your radiant heart to me, you made known to me the manner and quality of your enlightening more clearly than to anyone else so far, as may be inferred by those who have read your writings.

Assuredly, you have weighed my request and your generosity in your honest scales, judging it right to open the chamber of love to the eye of love and to make me a participant of that exultation, of that delightful secret, not as a spy but as one who takes delight in your joy. You willingly did this for me because the door is opened to the one who knocks [cf. Matt 7.7]. Why, therefore, should my heart not exult in the Lord, my mouth be filled with jubilation, my lips rejoice, since I was uttering with my mouth, proclaiming with my lips, and turning over in my heart those words that were sent out especially to me, words which you could not have learned from your own self, nor from any other human being, but which could only have come in a supernal vision?

Now, however—to turn from my expression of admiration for you to speak, for a moment, of myself—I was burning with no little embarrassment, and my heart was palpitating with fear when, in one part of your letter, the weakness of my conscience and the inconstancy of my character were laid bare, while, in another—with me reading these words in open public—you called me, variously, "servant of God" or "son of God" or "worthy knight." Venerable mother, may almighty God have mercy on you! What kind of burden have you imposed on me, an inept and indolent creature? You will see in what spirit you have made such pronouncements.

Where, after all, do such qualities as these appear in me? If anyone but you were saying such things, I would reject them out of hand, accounting them as lies or mere flattery. Yet I do not dare to contradict your words, which flow, as you assert, from the supernal fountain. Still, I suffer some little agony of turmoil about myself within my being when I contrast what I hear from you with what I know to be true about myself. Nevertheless, because I believe that you are neither willing nor able to lie, let it be done to me according to thy word [cf. Luke 1.38], whatsoever my real condition. That is to say, with the Lord's help may I become a servant, serving with my whole heart, and a son in my devoted imitation of His Son. And, since the life of man on this earth is a state of war, may I become an approved knight of God, recovering from my weakness and made strong in battle, fighting manfully against vice and the demons that instigate vice. And so that I may not lack your aid also in this battle, pray to Him, Who "knoweth the high afar off" [Ps 137.6] and regards humble things up close, both in heaven and on earth, pray to Him that He not allow my heart to be destroyed by a calamitous outcome, on the one hand, nor, on the other, to exult when the battle goes my way. And pray that He keep my eyes from being lifted up in pride with a desire to walk among the mighty or meddle in things too high for me [cf. Ps 130.1], but may He make me humble and poor in spirit, trembling at His word [cf. Is 66.2], so that He may deign to gather me with the meek of the earth and regard me with compassion.

Meanwhile, when day was beginning to turn to evening, Lord Siger returned home, and when he saw me, smiled graciously and directed to me the greetings you had entrusted to him. And when he learned that I had read your letter, he said, "I pray that you will expound it to me in French, lest I be like the ass that carries the wine but does not taste it." And although he kept urging his request, with some little difficulty I got him to put the matter off until the next day, for it was already evening. Later, seeking to fulfill his desire to the best of my ability, I attempted to satisfy him in this difficult matter, in the presence of a number of people, both clergy and laity. Then, awe seized everyone, and, filled with wonder, they all gave thanks to Wisdom, and to the Spirit that was speaking through its instrument, that is, your mouth. All of these people, of varying rank and age, kept insisting—indeed demanding—that I fulfill this difficult task of translation, unwilling though I was. Yet how gladly they listened to that letter of yours, how eagerly they had copies made, how enthusiastically they read and praised it—not just individual readers but almost the entire church!

Hence it is that when that letter was read to Lord Robert, former abbot of Val-Roi and a man of great reputation and learning, he sat quietly, shaking his head time and again. He was so moved that he burst out in a way that could scarcely have been anticipated, though still with dignity, and he testified that the words he had heard could have come from none other than the Holy Spirit. "I believe," he said, "that not even the greatest theologians in France today, however great their intelligence, could completely comprehend the power and depth of some of the words found in this letter, except through the revelation of that same Spirit which inspired them. They prattle with parched heart and blathering cheeks, reveling in questions and battles, from which quarrels arise. And, all the while, they don't have the slightest idea what they are talking about. Thus they enmesh themselves—and others—inextricably in the entangling coils of contention.[2] But this blessed lady, constantly disciplined, as I hear tell, by the whip of infirmity, and restrained by her own will, contemplates the one thing that is alone necessary, the glory of the Blessed Trinity, in the utmost simplicity of heart. Mild and gentle in heart, she drinks

---

2. Here, as in Volmar's letter, one can see the friction developing between the old monastic order and the new spirit developing in the universities, which will come to full flower in the age of scholasticism.

from that fullness within herself and pours it out of herself to relieve the thirst of those who thirst."

Another person[3] added comments that quite agreed with this. "It is nothing new or unusual," he said, "for the souls of men to be illumined by the various gifts of the Holy Spirit. As the Apostle says, 'every one hath his proper gift from God; one after this manner, and another after that' [I Cor 7.7], and in another passage, 'now there are diversities of graces, but the same Spirit' [I Cor 12.4], 'dividing to every one according as he will' [I Cor 12.11]. A new sign of sanctification at length shone forth among our predecessors, about which we solemnly sing:

> Today He has bestowed
> upon Christ's apostles
> a singular gift,
> unheard of
> in any generation.

This refers, of course, to the flickering tongues of fire sitting on each one of the apostles, from whose mouths came forth all manner of tongues [cf. Acts 2.3–4]. Just so, beyond doubt, this too is a new kind of illumination by which this lady is granted clear sight. And unlike others who see divine things in sleep, or in dreams, or in ecstasy, she perceives those things shown to her, wondrous to say, fully awake, irradiated, as she herself declares, in a certain eternal light, which she calls the shadow of the Living Light. And during such visions, she is always alert and self-controlled. Furthermore, if she sees certain things in enigmatic terms, there are many more that she observes with a pure, veracious understanding, with all mystic appearances removed, and she is so much at peace in either mode that she cannot be drawn away from the contemplation of inner things by noticing exterior things.

---

3. Critics believe that this is Guibert himself.

"Moreover, this gift of hers exceeds the illumination of all others, because the words which she hears in those visions have the double effect of fire in her: she both burns and shines in them. And, also, in that Light (by which she has been illumined from childhood, and which she still enjoys to this day) her spirit is exalted and expanded, since she not only gains an understanding of the Holy Scriptures, but is also made capable of seeing into certain (if not all) works of men, however far distant they are from her. The blessed Gregory testifies to the uniqueness of her gift by his evidence to the contrary, for he maintains that the spirit of prophecy does not always irradiate the minds of the prophets, citing two passages from the Scripture in proof: in one David asks Nathan about the building of the temple, and Nathan at one moment grants, at the next forbids it [cf. II Sam 7.2ff]. It is clear that he would not have done this if the spirit were continually present. In the other passage Elisha speaks to Giezi concerning the Sunamite: 'Let her alone for her soul is in anguish, and the Lord hath hid it from me, and hath not told me' [II Kings 4.27]. And since 'deep calleth on deep' [Ps 41.8] in the height of divine revelations, it follows that this illumination in her is totally new, and surpasses all others up to the present time. For on those rare occasions when she enters the mystery of the Living Light, as she herself testifies, she seems to herself to be completely transformed, as it is written 'thy youth shall be renewed like the eagle's' [Ps 102.5]. And just as she feels herself to be a young girl again, she completely forgets all troubles that have befallen her—infirmity, sadness, pain, and the feebleness of her advanced years—and carried away by the sweetness of the symphonic harmony, a delight inexpressible to her and inconceivable to us (since, although well-known to her, it surpasses our senses), she, mentally, grows quiet and sleeps in peace in that Light, while, physically, she is fully awake.

"Moreover, returning to ordinary life from the melody of that internal concert, she frequently takes delight in causing those sweet melodies which she learns and remembers in that spiritual harmony to reverberate with the sound of voices, and, remembering God, she makes a feast day from what she remembers of that spiritual music. Furthermore, she composes hymns in praise of God and in honor of the saints, and has those melodies, far more pleasing than ordinary human music, publicly sung in church. Who has ever heard such things said about any other woman?

"And so what does it matter if she is ignorant of the liberal arts and grammar? And what does it matter if she does not know anything about the agreement of cases, inflections, genders, numbers, degrees, or anything else of that kind? She is, for all that, refulgent with such extraordinary learning, and possesses such a great understanding of the Scriptures that, as we read of St. Martin, she is ready to answer Biblical questions on the spot. And in ordinary conversation she is articulate and lucid, always ready to answer whatever is asked of her. Nor has it been her custom to do this impudently and petulantly, as one might, but, quite the contrary, when she has a ready answer, she pours forth what has been distilled to her without delay. If, however, she is not prepared to answer immediately, she prays, with seemly delay and humble devotion, for things which are unclear to her or of which she is ignorant to be opened up to her by the One Who reveals mysteries. And when she receives what she seeks from the largess of the One Who breathes where and when He will [cf. John 3.8], in absolute faith she imparts to those who question her the abundance of blessing she has received—without ill-will or refusal.

"This woman abundantly proves St. Gregory's dictum that 'the gift of the Holy Spirit is not constrained by law.' And rightly so, since she neither allows herself to be separated from the One because of the love of another, nor to be bound by the law by subjecting herself to the power of a man through marriage. Rather, called to freedom of spirit, she keeps the faith to that One alone, to Whom she has proved herself and Whom she desires to please with a holy body and spirit. In this way, she surpasses other women, who bear the burdens of marriage.

"The Apostle does not allow a woman to teach in church [cf. I Tim 2.12], but, through the gift of the Spirit, this woman is absolved from that prohibition, and, having been taught by His instruction, she has come to know that Scripture very well in her heart: 'Blessed is the one whom thou shalt instruct, O Lord: and shalt teach out of thy law' [Ps 93.12]. And ignorant perhaps in word, but not in knowledge, she teaches many through her sound doctrine, pouring forth abundantly from her two breasts, as it were, the milk of consolation for the ignorant and the wine of correction for the strong. But although the divine anointing teaches her within about all things, and commands her, as we find in her writings, to disclose faithfully and openly for the instruction of her hearers what the Spirit intimates to her secretly, she nevertheless bears in mind her sex, her appropriate condition, and especially the Apostle's aforementioned prohibition. She is obedient to the Spirit, and does not contradict the Apostle sent by the Spirit, but, rather, she educates the Church with books and sermons wholly consonant throughout to the Catholic faith, teaching in the Church, but not after the fashion of those who are accustomed to harangue the people.

"The Apostle also commands women to cover their heads with veils [cf. I Cor 11.5ff], not only out of respect for discipline but also as a commendation either to some mystery or to the submission they are obliged to observe. Yet this woman is not obliged to wear the kind of veil that wives commonly wear, although some kind of veil is required. For in her great loftiness, she transcends the lowly condition of women. And she is to be compared to the most eminent of men, for 'beholding the glory of the Lord with unveiled face, she is transformed into the same image from brightness unto brightness, as by the Spirit of the Lord' [II Cor 3.18].

"How appropriate 'from brightness unto brightness' is for one whose spirit is always illuminated by the various shifts and welcome approaches of that Light, which, as we said above, she has learned to call the shadow of the Living Light, and, carried off into that same Light of Life, she gives thanks to God, saying, 'Thou shalt fill me with joy with thy countenance' [Ps 15.11], and 'the light of thy countenance, O Lord, is signed upon us' [Ps 4.7], 'for with thee is the fountain of light; and in thy light I see light' [Ps 35.10]. When, on those rare occasions, she is inundated and carried off by the radiance of that Living Light, she is so totally, miraculously, changed, as her friends as well as her writings testify, that from the very gain in spiritual and bodily strength, one can tell to the minute when that fiery torrent flows into her, of which torrent it is written, 'suddenly there came a sound from heaven, and like a torrent of wind it filled the whole house' [Acts 2.2], and 'A divine fire came, a fire not burning but illuminating, blazing but not consuming, and it found the hearts of the disciples to be clean vessels, and it imparted to them the gifts of the spirit.' Then she becomes more lively in spirit, more spirited in expression, sharper in perception, readier with her words, and more agile in her body. Thus although at other times she never went anywhere without being assisted by one or two nuns, at that time, miraculously strengthened, she walks easily without any assistance whatsoever, to the great wonder and joy of those who are present.

"But why should one wonder if by that Majesty, by whose nod all things move, she is able to do that which, by herself, she is not able to do? Do not the words of that Lady, blessed above all women, apply here, if not literally, at least as a very clear sign? That Lady, through whom the restored human race rejoices, said while gestating our salvation in her womb, 'Daughters of Jerusalem, why do you marvel at me? This mystery which you see is divine.'

"Another miraculous thing is reported of her, which her friends, who have frequently witnessed it, assert to be true: sometimes she fails to obey a divine command to write something or to go out to other monasteries, far or near, in order to admonish the faithful or, where necessary, to correct certain problems. And whether this failure of hers is due, God forbid, to sloth or obstinacy, or whether it is to be blamed on feminine dread or virginal shamefastness (lest it be said that she did it through presumption or through her own will), whatever the reason, she is immediately scourged doubly by the whip of illness, and by a clear sign she utterly closes up the mouths of those who speak evil of her [cf. Ps 62.12], for her body suddenly becomes so totally rigid that it appears not to be human flesh but unbending wood, and this rigidity is never relaxed until she fulfills those commands."

After your letter was read, and he saw the astonishment of those who heard it, he became not an envious, but a well-wishing preacher of your glories, reverend mother, and he spoke of grace divinely bestowed upon you, making those listeners even more fervent in praise of God and in admiration of you. Everyone agreed that that same God, Who is always marvelous in His saints [cf. Ps 67.36], was manifested in you. And by His gift and the glory of virginity, you shine unburnt in the middle of the Babylonian furnace [cf. Dan 3.19ff], and, having drunk of the fountain of life, you pour forth sweet honey and rich butter to us who hunger.

Now, concerning those things which many people say about you in our region, holy mother, this will suffice at present. For if I go beyond measure in this matter, someone who does not know my heart might think I am currying favor with you through flattering words, and you, either troubled by this praise or terrified by it, might become angry with me. Indeed, if I may speak the truth, it is better for you to be terrified than to be delighted, for it is certainly true that to wish to have a praiseworthy name without a praiseworthy life is certain damnation. That man of the highest perfection[4] says, "I do not consider that I have achieved anything" [Phil 3.13] in any Christian battle. Also it is written, "when a man hath

---

4. That is, St. Paul.

done, then he begins" [Ecclus 18.6]. Moreover, as a certain wise man says, praise of a man, if true, is a proclamation, if false, a condemnation. Thus it follows that nobody, although conscious of no crime or sin in himself, should take pride, but should fear. And anyone in a good situation should desire and seek more earnestly to have good work than to have a good name, and he should not boast in himself to his ruin, but in the Lord to his benefit, for not the one who commends himself but the one whom God commends is worthy [cf. II Cor 10.18].

Farewell in Christ, venerable mother, and keep me and those who are mindful of you in your prayers.

The Last, Bitter Controversy

In 1178, when she was eighty years old, with only one more year to live, Hildegard was caught up in an exceedingly bitter and acrimonious struggle, and, as a result, was forced to endure the greatest privation of her life. In that year she had allowed the body of a certain nobleman (whose name has not come down to us) to be buried in the consecrated grounds of Mount St. Rupert. At some point in his life, however, the man had been excommunicated, and, on this basis, the prelates of the archbishopric of Mainz demanded that Hildegard exhume the body and cast it out of holy ground. The Mainz prelates spoke for their archbishop, who was away in Rome at that time on official ecclesiastical business, and they went further, taking the extreme and excessive measure, in his name, of placing Mount St. Rupert under interdict until Hildegard complied with their order. Hildegard acknowledged that the man had indeed been excommunicated, but she argued (correctly and successfully, as it turned out) that he had been fully reconciled to the Church before his death. She went further than mere argument, however: she apparently went out and made sure that the grave was hidden so that she would not be taken unawares with the body being disinterred without her knowledge. The later, unsuccessful protocol for her canonization reports that she lifted her staff over the grave and, making the sign of the cross, caused it to disappear. Hildegard eventually won out in this contest of wills, by making contact with the archbishop and by *producing witnesses in proof of the man's absolution. But, in the meantime, she—and her community—suffered under the grievous restrictions of the interdict: the nuns were forbidden to hear mass, receive the Eucharist, or even sing the divine office. And anyone who knows the artistic spirit of this woman—poet and musician in her own right, composer of divine songs and hymns and creator of music—knows what a terrible affliction this latter deprivation was.*

The following letter is a forceful and compelling argument for the lifting of the interdict, incorporating within its framework her wondrous excursus on the mystical power of music to recapture the joyousness and beauty of paradise before the Fall. It was a signal and lovely performance—and it was totally ignored by the prelates of Mainz.

The interdict was lifted, at last, a few months before Hildegard's death.

Letter 72 ❧ to the Prelates at Mainz

By a vision, which was implanted in my soul by God the Great Artisan before I was born, I have been compelled to write these things because of the interdict by which our superiors have bound us, on account of a certain dead man buried at our monastery, a man buried without any objection, with his own priest officiating. Yet only a few days after his burial, these men ordered us to remove him from our cemetery. Seized by no small terror, as a result, I looked as usual to the True Light, and, with wakeful eyes, I saw in my spirit that if this man were disinterred in accordance with their commands, a terrible and lamentable danger would come upon us like a dark cloud before a threatening thunderstorm.

Therefore, we have not presumed to remove the body of the deceased inasmuch as he had confessed his sins, had received extreme unction and communion, and had been buried without objection. Furthermore, we have not yielded to those who advised or even commanded this course of action. Not, certainly, that we take the counsel of upright men or the orders of our superiors lightly, but we would not have it appear that, out of feminine harshness[1] we did injustice to the sacraments of Christ, with which this man had been fortified while he was still alive. But so that we may not be totally disobedient we have, in accordance with their injunction, ceased from singing the divine praises and from participation in Mass, as had been our regular monthly custom.

As a result, my sisters and I have been greatly distressed and saddened. Weighed down by this burden, therefore, I heard these words in a vision: "It is improper for you to obey human words ordering you to abandon the sacraments of the Garment of the Word of God, Who, born virginally of the Virgin Mary, is your salvation. Still, it is incumbent upon you to seek permission to participate in the sacraments from those prelates who laid the obligation of obedience upon you. For ever since Adam was driven from the bright region of paradise into the exile of this world on account of his disobedience, the conception of all people is justly tainted by that first transgression. Therefore, in accordance with God's inscrutable plan, it was necessary for a man free from all pollution to be born in human flesh, through whom all who are predestined to life might be cleansed from corruption and might be sanctified by the communion of his body so that he might remain in them and they in him for their fortification. That person, however, who is disobedient to the commands of God, as Adam was, and is completely forgetful of Him must be completely cut off from participation in the sacrament of His body, just as he himself has turned away from Him in disobedience. And he must remain so until, purged through penitence, he is permitted by the authorities to receive the communion of the Lord's body again. In contrast,

---

1. How cannily Hildegard plays to her masculine audience!

however, a person who is aware that he has incurred such a restriction not as a result of anything that he has done, either consciously or deliberately, may be present at the service of the life-giving sacrament, to be cleansed by the Lamb without sin, Who, in obedience to the Father, allowed Himself to be sacrificed on the altar of the cross that he might restore salvation to all."

In that same vision I also heard that I had erred in not going humbly and devoutly to my superiors for permission to participate in the communion, especially since we were not at fault in receiving that dead man into our cemetery. For, after all, he had been fortified by his own priest with proper Christian procedure, and, without objection from anyone, was buried in our cemetery, with all Bingen joining in the funeral procession. And so God has commanded me to report these things to you, our lords and prelates. Further, I saw in my vision also that by obeying you we have been celebrating the divine office incorrectly, for from the time of your restriction up to the present, we have ceased to sing the divine office, merely reading it instead. And I heard a voice coming from the Living Light concerning the various kinds of praises, about which David speaks in the psalm: "Praise Him with sound of trumpet: praise Him with psaltery and harp," and so forth up to this point: "Let every spirit praise the Lord" [Ps 150.3–5]. These words use outward, visible things to teach us about inward things. Thus the material composition and the quality of these instruments instruct us how we ought to give form to the praise of the Creator and turn all the convictions of our inner being to the same. When we consider these things carefully, we recall that man needed the voice of the living Spirit, but Adam lost this divine voice through disobedience. For while he was still innocent, before his transgression, his voice blended fully with the voices of the angels in their praise of God. Angels are called spirits from that Spirit which is God, and thus they have such voices by virtue of their spiritual nature. But Adam lost that angelic voice which he had in paradise, for he fell asleep to that knowledge which he possessed before his sin, just as a person on waking up only dimly remembers what he had seen in his dreams. And so when he was deceived by the trick of the devil and rejected the will of his Creator, he became wrapped up in the darkness of inward ignorance as the just result of his iniquity. God, however, restores the souls of the elect to that pristine blessedness by infusing them with the light of truth. And in accordance with His eternal plan, He so devised it that whenever He renews the hearts of many with the pouring out of the prophetic spirit, they might, by means of His interior illumination, regain some of the knowledge which Adam had before he was punished for his sin.

And so the holy prophets, inspired by the Spirit which they had received, were called for this purpose: not only to compose psalms and canticles (by which the hearts of listeners would be inflamed) but also to construct various kinds of musical instruments to enhance these songs of praise with melodic strains. Thereby, both through the form and quality of the instruments, as well as through the meaning of the words which accompany them, those who hear might be taught, as we said above, about inward things, since they have been admonished and aroused by outward things. In such a way, these holy prophets get beyond the music of this exile and recall to mind that divine melody of praise which Adam, in company with the angels, enjoyed in God before his fall.

Men of zeal and wisdom have imitated the holy prophets and have themselves, with human skill, invented several kinds of musical instruments, so that they might be able to sing for the delight of their souls, and they accompanied their singing with instruments played with the flexing of the fingers, recalling, in this way, Adam, who was formed by God's finger, which is the Holy Spirit. For, before he sinned, his voice had the sweetness of all musical harmony. Indeed, if he had remained in his original state, the weakness of mortal man would not have been able to endure the power and the resonance of his voice.

But when the devil, man's great deceiver, learned that man had begun to sing through God's inspiration and, therefore, was being transformed to bring back the sweetness of the songs of heaven, mankind's homeland, he was so terrified at seeing his clever machinations go to ruin that he was greatly tormented. Therefore, he devotes himself continually to thinking up and working out all kinds of wicked contrivances. Thus he never ceases from confounding confession and the sweet beauty of both divine praise and spiritual hymns, eradicating them through wicked suggestions, impure thoughts, or various distractions from the heart of man and even from the mouth of the Church itself, wherever he can, through dissension, scandal, or unjust oppression.

Therefore, you and all prelates must exercise the greatest vigilance to clear the air by full and thorough discussion of the justification for such actions before your verdict closes the mouth of any church singing praises to God or suspends it from handling or receiving the divine sacraments. And you must be especially certain that you are drawn to this action out of zeal for God's justice, rather than out of indignation, unjust emotions, or a desire for revenge, and you must always be on your guard not to be circumvented in your decisions by Satan, who drove man from celestial harmony and the delights of paradise.

Consider too that just as the body of Jesus Christ was born of the purity of the Virgin Mary through the operation of the Holy Spirit so too the canticle of praise, reflecting celestial harmony, is rooted in the Church through the Holy Spirit. The body is the vestment of the spirit, which has a living voice, and so it is proper for the body, in harmony with the soul, to use its voice to sing praises to God. Whence, in metaphor, the prophetic spirit commands us to praise God with clashing cymbals and cymbals of jubilation [cf. Ps 150.5], as well as other musical instruments which men of wisdom and zeal have invented, because all arts pertaining to things useful and necessary for mankind have been created by

THE LAST, BITTER CONTROVERSY

the breath that God sent into man's body. For this reason it is proper that God be praised in all things.

And because sometimes a person sighs and groans at the sound of singing, remembering, as it were, the nature of celestial harmony, the prophet, aware that the soul is symphonic and thoughtfully reflecting on the profound nature of the spirit, urges us in the psalm [cf. Ps 32.2] to confess to the Lord with the harp and to sing a psalm to Him with the ten-stringed psaltery. His meaning is that the harp, which is plucked from below, relates to the discipline of the body; the psaltery, which is plucked from above, pertains to the exertion of the spirit; the ten chords, to the fulfillment of the law.

Therefore, those who, without just cause, impose silence on a church and prohibit the singing of God's praises and those who have on earth unjustly despoiled God of His honor and glory will lose their place among the chorus of angels, unless they have amended their lives through true penitence and humble restitution. Moreover, let those who hold the keys of heaven beware not to open those things which are to be kept closed nor to close those things which are to be kept open, for harsh judgment will fall upon those who rule, unless, as the apostle says [cf. Rom 12.8], they rule with good judgment.

And I heard a voice saying thus: Who created heaven? God. Who opens heaven to the faithful? God. Who is like Him? No one. And so, O men of faith, let none of you resist Him or oppose Him, lest He fall on you in His might and you have no helper to protect you from His judgment. This time is a womanish time, because the dispensation of God's justice is weak. But the strength of God's justice is exerting itself, a female warrior battling against injustice, so that it might fall defeated.

When the Mainz prelates ignored the previous eloquent letter and refused to lift the interdict, Hildegard wrote the following personal appeal to the archbishop, who was still detained in Rome on official Church business, laying out in detail the causes of the conflict and the steps she had taken to resolve it.

Letter 73 🌸 *to Christian, Archbishop of Mainz*

O most gentle father and lord, appointed to be Christ's representative as shepherd of the flock of the Church, we humbly give thanks to almighty God and to your paternal piety that you have received our letter compassionately, poor though we are, and that in your mercy you have deigned to send a letter to our superiors in Mainz on our behalf when we were sorely tried and perplexed. We give thanks also for the kind words expressed with your usual clemency, which (brought by Hermann, dean of the church of the Holy Apostles in Cologne) so consoled and cheered us in our trials and tribulations that we have run to you in all confidence, like daughters to their cherished father. Therefore, gracious lord, we your servants, who sit in the grief of our trials and tribulations and have humbly cast ourselves at your feet, now tearfully lay bare to you the full truth concerning the cause of our intolerable grief. We are confident that the fire of Love, which is God, will so inspire you that your paternal piety will deign to hear the cry of lament, which, in our tribulation, we raise to you.

O mild father, as I informed you earlier in a letter, a certain young man who was buried in our cemetery had been absolved from excommunication for some time before his death and had been fortified with all the sacraments of the Christian faith. When our superiors at Mainz ordered us to cast him out of our cemetery or else refrain from singing the divine offices, I looked, as usual, to the True Light, through which God instructed me that I was never to accede to this: one whom He had received from the bosom of the Church into the glory of salvation was by no means to be disinterred. For to do so against the will of His truth would bring great and terrible danger down upon us. Yet I would have humbly obeyed them, and would have willingly yielded up that dead man, excommunicated or not, to anyone whom they had sent in your name to enforce the inviolable law of the Church—if my fear of almighty God had not stood in my way.

Thus although we did cease singing the divine offices for some time (though not without great sorrow), the Mighty Judge, whose commands I have not dared to disobey, sent the true vision into my soul. And forced by this, despite a grievous illness, I went to our superiors in Mainz, where I presented in writing the words I had seen in the True Light, just as God Himself instructed me. Thus might they know the will of God in this matter. There, in their presence, I tearfully sought pardon, and with weeping and humility asked for their compassion. Yet their eyes were so clouded that they could not look at me with any trace of compassion, and so, full of tears, I departed from them.

But a great number of people did have pity for us, although, despite their good will, they could offer us no real assistance. Yet my faithful friend, the archbishop of Cologne, came to Mainz bringing with him a certain knight, a free man. And this man was willing to offer sufficient testimony that he and the afore-mentioned dead man had been partners in that transgression and that the two of them had likewise received absolution from excommunication, in the same place, and at the same hour, by the same priest. And that very priest was there present and verified the truth of this matter, and, acting in your name, obtained permission for us to celebrate the divine offices in security and peace until your return. Now, however, although we still have the utmost confidence in your compassion, most gracious lord, we have just received your letter from the synod forbidding us, once again, to celebrate those offices, a letter delivered to us by our superiors upon their return from Rome. Yet, having confidence in your paternal piety, I am assured that you never would have sent that letter if you had known the truth of the matter. And so, most gentle father, by the order which you yourself gave, we find ourselves again under that previous restriction and are suffering even greater grief and sadness.

Now, in a vision—and you have never, I remind you, given me trouble about my visions before—I have been ordered to say with heart and mouth: It is better for me to fall into the hands of men, than to abandon the command of my God [cf. Dan 13.23]. Therefore, most gentle father, for the love of the Holy Spirit and the piety owed to the eternal Father, who sent his Word into the womb of the Virgin to blossom there for the salvation of mankind, I beseech you not to look down upon the tears of your grieving and wailing daughters who out of fear of God are enduring the trials and perplexities of this unjust injunction. May the Holy Spirit be so poured out on you that you may be moved to compassion for us and so that at the end of your life you may in return receive compassion.

The archbishop responds positively to Hildegard's appeal, informing her that he has written the prelates at Mainz that she is to be allowed to celebrate the divine offices again. Nevertheless, he insists, as he was duty-bound to do, that evidence and witnesses be brought forward in proof of the dead man's absolution.

Letter 74 from Christian, Archbishop of Mainz

Christian, archbishop of Mainz by the grace of God, to Hildegard, revered lady and beloved in Christ, and to all the brides of Christ who serve God with her, with a prayer that they might ascend from virtue unto virtue and see the God of gods in Zion [cf. Ps 83.8].

Although in the wondrous and praiseworthy power of God and the mercy of our Savior, we are woefully inadequate, nay rather completely unworthy, yet, dearest lady in Christ, having the utmost confidence in your faithful prayers that we may be made worthy, we honor with our thanks Him from whom descends "every best gift, and every perfect gift...coming down from the Father of lights" [James 1.17]. For He has been pleased, and rightly so, with your soul and has illuminated it with His true and unfathomable light, and his continuing grace has been granted to your saintly devotion, to sit with Mary at the feet of the Lord [cf. Luke 10.39] and receive visions of the heavenly Jerusalem.

Dearest lady in Christ, these obvious signs of your holy life and such amazing testimonies to the truth oblige us to obey your commands and to pay especial heed to your entreaties. Thus we are rightly obliged to cast the gaze of our heart to whatever we know has been granted to your saintly prayers. And having the greatest confidence in your sanctity (next only to that we owe God), we hope, through the sacred odor of your prayers, to attain God's eternal grace. We also hope that this sinful soul of ours, made the more acceptable through your saintly intercession, will obtain the mercy of its Creator.

Hence, with regard to the tribulation and affliction which you and yours are enduring because of the suspension of the divine offices, the clearer your innocence in this matter becomes to us, the more firmly we sympathize with you. Nevertheless, the Church held that the man buried in your churchyard had incurred the sentence of excommunication while he was alive, and although some doubt remained concerning his absolution, the fact that you disregarded the outcry of the clergy and acted as if this would cause no scandal in the Church was a very dangerous act, since the statutes of the holy fathers are inviolable. You should have waited for definitive proof based on the suitable testimony of good men in the presence of the Church.

Yet we wholeheartedly sympathize with your affliction, as is only right, and therefore we have written back to the church at Mainz to this effect: we grant you the privilege of celebrating the divine offices again, on the condition that proof of the dead man's absolution has been established by the testimony of reliable men. In the meantime, saintly lady, if we have caused you annoyance in this matter, either out of guilt or ignorance, we earnestly beseech you not to withhold your compassion from one who seeks pardon. May you deign to pray the Father of mercies to present us unblemished to your sight and to the church at Mainz, for the glory of God and the honor of your church and for the salvation of our soul. May the Lord preserve your wholeness and holiness.

Songs and Hymns

This final document, although a "meditation" rather than a "letter," is a fitting conclusion to this work, for it is, in effect, a letter to the divine, consisting, as it does, almost wholly of songs and poems to the Trinity and the Holy Virgin.

Letter 75   *A Meditation*

> O Word of the Father,
> You are the light of the first dawn
> In the sphere of the circle
> Accomplishing all things with Your divine power.
> O Foreknowledge of God,
> You foresaw all Your works
> Just as You willed them,
> With Your omniscience
> Remaining hidden in the midst of Your might.
> And You were active

Like a wheel
Which encircles all things
And has neither beginning
Nor end.[1]

Although the fraudulent devil deceived the man God had formed, there was a power in God, in which He delighted, but which the ancient serpent for all his searching neither knew nor had a taste of. This power is the beautiful form of the Son of God, Who overcame the devil in the abyss [cf. Apoc 17.8], and drew man's breath to Himself, and ripped open the belly of the devil. Thus by His own wounds, He freed man from the devil, whose bowels he had passed through, and snatching him from the prison of hell, He adorned him again with the wings of a white cloud.[2]

Therefore, O mankind, rejoice, because God made you to be the battle flag of holy divinity, and He gained the victory through you when He broke down the gates of hell. Your created form was at the center of all creation, so that all the angelic host saw you and marveled. And so He sealed you with the harmony of heaven in angelic victory, through which you will perfect the forms of the virtues in your battles.

Rejoice therefore, O mankind, and do not mislead yourselves into mockery through ignorance, as if you were not already greatly honored, because God made you such that He fully achieved all His miracles in you. For, first, the mist of death came into the world through the form of a woman, so that Eve changed all the joy of those who give birth into pain, when she went into exile, after the serpent, who had tempted her into evil, had deceived her. Then, that mist of death was cast out through another feminine form. For God had foreseen in the

---

1. Here and elsewhere in this meditation we have employed the stanzaic patterns for the songs established by Barbara Newman in *Symphonia*.
2. This is, of course, a description of the Harrowing of Hell.

time before time that the devil would choke off life through a woman, and so in His wisdom He built a tower so lofty that He brought forth other life through another woman, who was chaste and innocent.

Therefore, O Wisdom, heaven and the angels adore you, and all the heavenly host marvels at you, saying: Oh! Oh! all the miracles of God arose from "the slime of the earth" [Gen 2.7], so that a new sun came forth, and a new light shone out, and a new song resounded among us. Wherefore, O Wisdom, praise be to you, because you found another woman, the Virgin Mary, that the serpent could not deceive, and she has crowned all the human race, so that from now on the devil will be unable to delude man as he did before. For in her pain Eve was the mother of all weeping, but in Mary joy resounded with harp and harmony. For she says to her Son regarding virginity:

> O my well-beloved Son,
> Whom I bore in my womb
> By the might of that ever-turning wheel
> Of holy divinity,
> That created me
> And ordered all my limbs,
> And in my womb
> Established
> Every kind of music
> In all the flowers of all the tones.
> Now, virgins in a vast throng
> Follow me and You,
> O my well-beloved Son.
> Deign
> To save them by Your aid.

And these virgins say: We walk in God, and all of us follow you, attending the order of angels. We have come forth as moisture from the earth, and we embrace You, O Son of the holy betrothal. Therefore,

O our sweet Lover,
O You Who embrace us sweetly!
Help us to preserve
Our virginity.

We were born in the dust
Alas, alas!
And in the sin of Adam,
And so it is difficult to refuse
The taste of the forbidden fruit.
But You, O Christ, our Savior, lift us up.

With hearts afire, we long to follow You,
But, O how difficult it is for us miserable creatures,
To imitate You, King of the angels,
Without blemish, without guilt.

Still, we trust in You
Because you long to seek again the jewel
In the corruption.

Now, we call out to You,
Bridegroom, Consoler,
To You Who redeemed
Us on the cross.

Through Your blood,
We have been joined to You
In betrothal,
Refusing a husband,
And choosing You,
O Son of God.

O most beautiful form,
O sweetest fragrance
Of the most delectable delights,
We always sigh for You
In this tear-filled exile.
When can we see You?
When can we stay with You?

We are in the world,
But You are always in our thoughts;
We embrace You in our hearts
As if You were here with us.

O Mighty Lion,
You burst forth from heaven,
Descending into the hall of the Virgin.
You destroyed death
And raised up life in a golden city.

Grant us to join with her
And to remain in You,
O sweetest Bridegroom,
For You snatched us from the jaws of the devil,
Who seduced our first parent.

And defend those also, we pray, who, even after carnal knowledge of a man, now follow You with great love, defend them from those who besiege them, for they cry out to You:

O Father of all,
O King and Ruler of all people,
You Who established us in the rib of the first mother,
The one who brought the great Ruin upon us.

And we have followed her
Into exile on our own account,
Joining ourselves to her grief.

O noblest Father,
In our great zeal we run to You,
And through penitence, precious and sweet,
Which comes to us through You,
We sigh to You,
And after our grief,
We devoutly embrace You.

O most glorious,
And most beautiful Christ,
Resurrection of life,
Because of You, we have left
The fertile lover we had married.
And, now, we embrace You
In divine love
Through the virginal branch of Your nativity.
And we have joined ourselves to You in a way
Different from the way we coupled in the flesh.

Help us to persevere
And to rejoice with You
And never to be parted from You.

O mighty Father,
We are in great need.
Now, therefore, we beseech You,
Through Your Word,
Through Which You established us replete

SONGS AND HYMNS

> With all that we need,
> To please look upon us,
> O Father, as befits You,
> So that, by Your aid,
> We do not fail,
> And that Your name be not forgotten among us.
> And through Your own name, we ask:
> Please help us.

And again, a voice from heaven said:

> O mankind,
> Created by God,
> You have been built in great holiness,
> Because Holy Divinity through humility
> Penetrated the heavens.
> O what great goodness it is
> That the Godhead shone in the slime of the earth
> And that the angels who minister to God
> See God in humanity.

But O what a strange thing it is that ashes lying in filth and sorely wounded by their sins refuse to look to God. For the Word of the Father "was made flesh" [John 1.14] for the sake of mankind. Therefore, let all people rejoice and with piteous voices mourn their sins, and turn to Him Who for their sake arrayed Himself in flesh, but without sin, so that He could cleanse away their guilt.

Now, all of you, most beloved, embrace this noble youth and love Him with great reverence, for He washed you in His blood [cf. Apoc 1.5], and He shows you the way to penitence for your sins, and healing for your wounds.

And again a voice resounded from heaven: O, you, you vile footstool, flee, flee! Steep ascents will give forth the fragrance of aromatic plants. Woe, woe, secular concerns! For the earth will hide herself, because the Living Eye Which sees all things will strike her on her jaw! The Spirit rejoices, but, O, O, the unhappy earth weeps for itself: Ah, ah! In this present time, she has places full of windows because of the deception of the ancient serpent, but the rending of the veil of God's temple has not yet come [cf. Matt 27.51; Mark 15.38].

> O virgin Church,
> Now is the time of mourning,
> Because the savage wolf
> Has dragged your children
> From your side.
> O woe unto the crafty serpent!
> But O how precious is the blood
> Of the Savior,
> Who with the banner of the King
> Has betrothed the Church to Himself.
> Therefore, He seeks
> Her children.

> Now let the maternal heart
> Of the Church rejoice,
> For in the symphony of heaven
> Her children
> Have been gathered into her bosom.
> Hence, O loathsome serpent,
> You have been confounded,
> For those you were confident you held
> In your bowels
> Now blaze in the blood of the Son of God.
> Therefore, praise be to You,
> King Most High!

O *orzchis*[3] Church,
Girt with the armor of God,
Adorned with hyacinth,
You are the *caldemia* of the wounds *loifolum*
And the city of all knowledge.
O, O you are *crizanta*
In the supernal music,
And you are a *chorzta* jewel.

And again I heard a voice from heaven, saying:

O might of eternity,
You Who arranged all things in Your heart,
By Your Word were all things created,
As You willed,
And Your Word
Clothed Himself in flesh
In that form
Which was taken from Adam.

And thus His garment
Was cleansed
By His great pain.

O, how great is the kindness of the Savior
Who liberated all things
By His Incarnation,

    3. In this brief song, Hildegard incorporates five words from her own *lingua ignota* ("unknown language"), the first and only time she employed that strange, artificial vocabulary in a literary work. We have let the original forms stand in the text. But information from other manuscripts indicates that they should be glossed as follows: *orzchis*, "immense"; *caldemia*, "aroma" or "fragrance"; *loifolum*, "of the people"; *crizanta*, "ornate" or "anointed"; *chorzta*, "flashing" or "gleaming."

> Which His divinity breathed forth,
> Free from the bondage of sin.

And:

> O spilled blood,
> You Who resounded on high
> When all the elements
> Entwined themselves
> Into a pitiable voice
> With trembling,
> Because the blood of their Creator
> Touched them,
> Cleanse Your children of their wounds
> With Your anointing oil.
>
> O Shepherd of souls,
> O earliest Voice
> Through Which all creatures were created,
> Now, Father, may it please You
> To free us from our distresses
> And our feebleness.

For a certain one arose from earth, whose voice resounded on high, a bright star crying out to mankind passionately that they must be penitent for their unrighteous works.[4] For God was mindful that through penitence for their ill-deeds He would re-create mankind in a new way. Therefore, let the heavens listen and let the earth tremble, because God receives penitent mankind, and because all the angels venerate Him with their praises. Therefore, woe to the person who spurns a sinner, because the Son of God has redeemed him by His blood [cf. Apoc 5.9], and accepts his repentance.

---

4. That is, John the Baptist.

First, the work of the Word of God encountered Him through His voice and so was created. Then, the Word set walls to construct an edifice, and so the world came into being. Then, the Eye of God looked at the form of man and sent into him the breath of life [cf. Gen 2.7] and filled his heart with knowledge. And so heaven was full, with eyes on all sides, and so served its Lord. Ah! Then, that old roarer, the devil [cf. I Pet 5.8], said within himself: Woe, woe! All the creation of God flashes like lightning, and none remains with me. And so from his mouth he breathed forth something like a sea, black and incorporeal, and directed it to mankind. Then, the Word of God saw that a cloud had covered His creation, and so He came into unplowed earth, that is, into the most noble Virgin, from whom He took on flesh, and so He cleansed mankind of that black sea and confounded the ancient serpent. Thus:

> O flowering branch
> Standing in your nobility
> Like breaking dawn:
> Now, rejoice and be glad
> and deign to free your weak followers
> From their sinful ways.
> Stretch out your hand
> To raise them up.

> Hail, nobly born,
> Glorious, and virginal girl!
> The beloved of chastity,
> The substance of sanctity,
> Pleasing to God.
> For God suffused you,
> And the supernal Word
> Clothed Himself with flesh in you.

You are the white lily
Which, before any other creature,
God looked upon.

O fairest and sweetest,
How greatly God delighted in you,
When He embraced you
With His heat
So that His Son
Was nurtured at your breast.

Your womb was full of joy
When all the harmony of heaven resounded your praise,
Because you, a virgin, carried the Son of God,
And since your purity was radiant in God.

Your heart was full of joy
Like the grass watered by dew
And made green by it.
Thus it happened to you,
O mother of all joy.

Now, let the whole Church glow with joy
And resound in harmony,
for the sweet Virgin,
Mary, worthy of all praise,
Mother of God.

Again, hail:

O rod and crown
Of the king's purple,
You are like a breastplate
In your chamber.

Burgeoning, you flowered forth
In a way different
From the way that Adam
Brought forth the whole human race.

Hail, hail! from your womb
Another life came forth
Of which Adam had despoiled
His children.

O flower, you did not blossom from the dew
Nor from drops of rain,
Nor from the air flying over you,
But the divine brightness
Brought you forth on the most noble bough.
O bough, on the first day
Of creation God had foreseen
Your blossoming.

And for His Word
He made you, O praiseworthy Virgin,
the golden medium.

O how great
In its might is the side of a man
From which God brought forth woman.
He made her the mirror
Of all loveliness
And the embrace
Of all His creation.

And so heavenly instruments sound in harmony
And the whole earth stands in amazement,

O Mary, worthy of all praise,
Because God loved you dearly.

O how much we must mourn and wail
Because sin and sorrow,
Through the serpent's wiles,
Flowed into woman.

For that very woman
That God established as the mother of all
Tore at her womb
With the wounds of her ignorance
And brought forth grief abundant
For her race.

But, O dawn,
From your womb
A new Sun came forth,
Who wiped away every sin of Eve,
And through you brought forth a blessing greater
Than the harm Eve had done to mankind.

Therefore, O Lady of our salvation,
You who brought forth
A new light for the human race:
Gather unto the harmony of heaven
Your Son's members.[5]

And, again, I heard a voice from heaven, saying: Behold, O golden might, how glorious You are, for You came forth in the first sound so that all the elements received life, and, afterward, You

---

5. That is, all the faithful.

tasted sanctity in Abel, because he poured out his innocent blood, and, then, in the ark of Noah You revealed new miracles when all the earth was stripped of its creatures. O Wisdom, You brought forth a new juice from the earth, and, in Abraham, you caused the name of the holy Trinity to be worshiped, and you gave to him circumcision, which announced the Incarnation of the Lord.

O star! In your brightness you revealed One more beautiful than all the children of mankind [cf. Ps 44.3], so that the magi worshiped the Son of God even as He was at the breast [cf. Matt 2.11], and so that all the virtues shone radiant from His face when He summoned anew all the sons of humankind, for all the elements and all the children of mankind saw the Word of God in the face of a human being.

Listen, therefore, O mankind, and say: "I fail to emulate Him, and I have opposed Him in my very being. Woe, woe, for this sin by which I have condemned myself."

Therefore, O God, You Who made man according to Your likeness and image [cf. Gen 1.26], in Him you perfected all good and crushed underfoot all wickedness, and You broke the gates of hell, and freed many souls: by the merits of these Your powers free Your faithful, who have completed in full the demands of their own will, but who still, from time to time, have looked to You in faith. And

> O You, fire of the Spirit, Paraclete,
> Life of the life of every creature,
> Holy are You for giving life to the forms,
> Holy are You for anointing
> Those who have been desperately wounded,
> Holy are You for cleansing
> Festering wounds.
>
> O Breath of holiness,
> O Fire of divine love,

O sweet taste in the breasts of men,
And anointment of hearts
In the sweet fragrance of the virtues.
O clearest fount,
In which we contemplate
That God gathers those who are estranged
And seeks those who are lost.

O Breastplate of life
And hope of the knitting of all our members,
O Sash of honor:
Save the blessed.

Watch over those who are made captive
By the enemy,
And loosen the bonds of those
Whom divine power wills to save.

O mightiest Way
You Who have penetrated all things
On high and on earth
And in all the depths,
You justly gather all people.

From You, the clouds flow, the ether flies,
From You, the rocks have their moisture,
From You, the waters bring forth their rills,
From You, the earth exudes its viridity.

You continually instruct the learned
Making them joyful

By the inspiration of Wisdom.
Therefore, praise be to You,
Who are the sound of praise,
And the joy of life,
Hope and mighty honor,
Bestowing gifts of light.

O fiery Spirit, praise to You,
Who with timbrel and harp
Bring forth Your music.

Enkindled by You, the minds of men blaze,
And the tabernacles of their spirits
House their might.
Thence the will arises
And imparts its taste to the soul,
And its lamp is desire.

Understanding calls to You with the sweetest sound
And prepares places of abode for You
With rationality,
Which brings forth golden works.

You always have the sword ready
To cut away that
Which the deadly fruit
Brings forth through homicide,
Foulest of crimes,

When a cloud rules over
The will and desires;

In those the soul flies,
And circles all about.

But the mind binds
the will and desires.
But when the soul rises
And seeks to see the eye of evil
and the jaws of sin,
You quickly burn it in the fire,
According to Your will.

But when rationality herself
Falls prostrate
Through wicked deeds,
You, according to Your will,
Bind her and restrain her and bring her back
Overwhelming her with trials.

But when evil
Unsheathes its sword against You,
You break into its heart,
Just as You did to the first, lost angel,
When You cast the tower of his pride
Into hell.

And there You raised
Another tower amid the publicans and sinners
Who confess their sins to You
And all their misdeeds.

And so all creatures,
Which have life from You praise You,

Because You are the ointment beyond price
For open, festering wounds,
And You transform them into rarest gems.

Now deign to gather
mankind to Yourself,
And direct us to straight paths.

Select Bibliography

Translations

Baird, Joseph L., and Radd Ehrman, trans. *The Letters of Hildegard of Bingen*. 3 vols. New York: Oxford University Press, 1994–2004.

Bowie, Fiona, and Oliver Davies. *Hildegard of Bingen: Mystical Writings*. New York: Crossroad, 1990.

Feiss, Hugh, trans. *The Life of the Saintly Hildegard—Written by the Monks Gottfried of Disibodenberg and Theoderic of Echternach*. Toronto: Peregrina, 1996.

Hart, Columba, and Jane Bishop, trans. *Hildegard of Bingen: Scivias*. New York: Paulist Press, 1990.

Notable Scholarly Works

Dronke, Peter. *Women Writers of the Middle Ages*. Cambridge: Cambridge University Press, 1984.

Flanagan, Sabina. *Hildegard of Bingen: A Visionary Life*. London: Routledge, 1989.

Newman, Barbara. *Sister of Wisdom: St. Hildegard's Theology of the Feminine*. Berkeley: University of California Press, 1987.

———, ed. and trans. *Symphonia. A Critical Edition of the Symphonia armonie celestium revelationum*. Ithaca: Cornell University Press, 1988.

SELECT BIBLIOGRAPHY

Fiction

Lachmann, Barbara. *The Journal of Hildegard of Bingen: A Novel.* New York: Bell Tower, 1993.

Ulrich, Ingeborg. *Hildegard of Bingen: Mystic, Healer, Companion of the Angels.* Trans. Linda M. Maloney. Collegeville, Minn.: Liturgical Press, 1993.

Index

Acta, 13
Adelbert of St. Disibod, 30
Adelheid, 41, 50, 51
Alexander III, pope, 120, 122
Anastasius IV, pope, 16
Arnold, Archbishop of Trier, 91, 94

Barbarossa. *See* Frederick I
Bernard of Clairvaux, 7, 15, 16, 17, 20, 117

Cathars, 90, 113
Christian, Archbishop of Mainz, 161, 164

Disibod, Mount St., 3, 13, 15, 29, 32, 35, 36
Dronke, Peter, 13

Eleanor of Aquitaine, 4, 78
Elisabeth of Schönau, 97, 98, 103

Eugenius III, pope, 18, 20, 21, 45, 64

Frederick I, 4, 5, 76–78, 116 n. 4

Gedolphus, Abbot of Brauweiler, 80, 84, 85
Gottfried of St. Disibod, 12
Guibert of Gembloux, 11, 13, 96, 135, 142

Hartwig, Archbishop of Bremen, 43, 48, 49
Heinrich, Archbishop of Mainz, 29, 41, 42, 45, 46
Helengerus, Abbot of St. Disibod, 32, 33, 120
Henry II of England, 5, 78
Hildegard of Bingen
   childhood experiences, 7, 8, 17–18
   exorcism, 80–91
   music, 4, 13, 156, 158–161

189

INDEX

Hildegard of Bingen (*continued*)
notion of weak, effeminate time, 12, 161
self-explanation of her means of "seeing," 9, 17, 138–139
visionary experiences, 8, 9–11, 16–17, 18

Irene, Empress of Greece, 5

Jutta of Sponheim, 3, 5, 6, 7

Kuno, Abbot of St. Disibod, 44

Lingua ignota, 11, 175 n. 3
Litterae ignotae, 11
Living Light, 12, 13, 14, 21, 22, 29, 42, 67, 105, 136, 139, 152, 158
shadow of the, 136, 138, 139, 152
Ludwig, Abbot of St. Eucharius, 129–132

Newman, Barbara, 13, 43 n. 3, 129 n. 2

Ordo virtutum, 14

Richardis von Stade, margravine, 29, 40, 41, 50
Richardis von Stade, nun, 15, 39, 40, 44, 45, 46, 47, 48, 51
Rupert, Mount St., 20, 24, 29, 40, 51, 120, 122, 155

Scivias, 8, 9, 13, 16, 20, 23, 24 n. 1, 39, 53, 139
MS, 9 n. 3
Sigewize, 85, 96

Tengswich of Andernach, 24, 26
Theodoric of Echternach, 12, 86–91

Vita, 12, 86
Volmar of St. Disibod, 7, 12, 15, 18, 36, 117, 120

Wezelinus, 92, 122